UP A FAMILY
TREE

UP A FAMILY
TREE

Teresa Bloomingdale

Doubleday & Company, Inc., Garden City, New York
1981

Library of Congress Cataloging in Publication Data

Bloomingdale, Teresa, 1930-
  Up a family tree.

  1. Family—Nebraska—Anecdotes, facetiae, satire, etc.   2. Family—Nebraska—Biography.   3.   Children—Nebraska—Anecdotes,
facetiae, satire, etc.   4. Children—Nebraska—Biography.   I. Title.
HQ555.N2B56   306.8′092′4   AACR2
ISBN 0-385-17032-7

Library of Congress Catalog Card Number 81-43053

To my mother and father
Helen Cooney Burrowes
and
Arthur (Bub) Burrowes
with much love.

ACKNOWLEDGMENTS

I would like to thank my daughter-in-law, Karen Bloomingdale, for typing the entire manuscript of this book without
once commenting on my atrocious spelling, and my daughter,
Mary Bloomingdale, for helping with the proofreading, and for
boosting me over many a writer's block with her repeated
offer to write a chapter on her parents.

My thanks, also, to my editor, Patricia Kossmann, for the
endless long-distance telephone conversations offering ideas
and inspiration, for her superb editing, and for her continuing reminder that raising ten kids can be both fun and funny.
(And if she reminds me one more time, I'm going to send her
all ten.)

And special thanks to my husband, Lee Bloomingdale, for
staying my husband throughout it all.

CONTENTS

INTRODUCTION:
THE FAMILY TREE

In the mid-1920s, when most Americans were enjoying the Jazz Age, dancing the Charleston, and drinking bootleg booze in an effort to forget the recent war and ignore the looming Depression, two Midwestern couples had little on their minds but romance.

In St. Joseph, Missouri, newspaperman Arthur (Bub) Burrowes was wooing the beautiful Helen Cooney, while in Omaha, Nebraska, oilman Arthur Bloomingdale had already wed Johanna Coady, the belle of Albia, Iowa.

For the next twenty-five years both couples lived in blissful ignorance of the frantic future, in which they would share the joys and sorrows, trials and tribulations, and continuing crises of the same set of grandchildren.

The first indication that branches of the two family trees would entangle came in 1952, when A. Lee Bloomingdale, only son of Art and 'Hanna, met Teresa Burrowes, second daughter of Bub and Helen, and was immediately smitten by her beauty, talent, and charm. (Vive la poetic license.) The young lawyer began a persistent and unrelenting courtship of the young lady (and a pox on future offspring who would suggest 'twas the other way 'round), which culminated in their wedding on July 2, 1955, in St. Francis Xavier Church, St. Joseph, Missouri.

The newlyweds settled in Omaha, where they planned to live out their lives in peace and prosperity. However, both the peace and the prosperity were indefinitely postponed by the subsequent arrival and continuing presence of the following persons:

Arthur Lee Bloomingdale III (b. 1956). A remarkable young man who survived not only the trauma of being the "first-born" but also the teasing brought on by that title: the Third. Young Lee spent his early childhood leading his brothers and sisters into mischief, then disappearing from the scene of the crime the moment the culprits got caught. (Why his siblings never killed him is beyond me.) In 1977, he married a lovely young lady named *Karen Marie Moore,* who joined our family willingly and voluntarily. (Despite this fact, she seems to be a sensible and intelligent person.)

John Joseph Bloomingdale (b. 1957). A handsome young man who spent the first twelve years of his life being his big brother's scapegoat, and the past twelve bearing the even more difficult burden of being his little brothers' idol. In his childhood, John's insatiable curiosity to find out how things work caused him to take apart (usually irreparably) everything he touched. It is not surprising, therefore, that John chose engineering for a career. (Let us hope he learns the difference between "assemble" and "disassemble.")

Michael Gerard Bloomingdale (b. 1958). Until the age of four, Mike was known as "the Fink." (Thank God; *somebody* had to keep Lee and John in line.) This tattler-toddler soon moved up to coconspirator and later, due to his mischievous mind, leader of the pack. Mike eventually turned into a charming, interesting adult, at which point, of course, he moved out.

James Burrowes Bloomingdale (b. 1959). After eighteen years of obeying the atrocious orders of his older brothers, taking the blame for the numerous misdemeanors of his younger brothers, and being subjected to the inhumane harassment of his three sisters, Jim found Marine Corps boot camp a breeze.

Mary Teresa Bloomingdale (b. 1961). The apple of her father's eye; the answer to her mother's prayers, Mary followed four brothers into this world and immediately assumed leadership. At the age of three she was luring her terrorist brothers to her tea parties with ladylike persuasion. . . . "Would you boys like to come to my tea party, or would you rather we all go tell Mom what you buried in Cunningham's back yard?" This sibling alliance eventually dissolved due to a language barrier: while the boys talk in American slang, Mary speaks only Shakespearean English. A product of the feminist generation, Mary is all for having a career, as long as it won't entail going to work.

Daniel Coady Bloomingdale (b. 1963). A brilliant, wise, and witty young man. (Just ask him. "No need to ask," says Dan. "It's self-evident.") How come a kid, who can rattle off the ruling monarchs of nineteenth-century Europe, the chronological adventures of the wily Odysseus, and the last twelve Heisman Trophy winners, can't remember that chemistry class was moved to Room 212?

Margaret Mary (Peggy) Bloomingdale (b. 1964). After a relatively uneventful childhood (unlike some of her siblings, Peg never set fire to the house, kidnapped the neighbor's cat, or forged her father's signature on report cards), Peg entered adolescence at the age of thirteen, decided she hated it, and accelerated herself into maturity. Thus, at sixteen, she had achieved the Impossible Dream: living like a teenager and enjoying it like an adult. Always popular with her peers, Peg won special tribute last year when she suggested a solution to the teenage summer-employment problem: "Why don't we all skip working this summer and just hang around the swimming pool?"

Ann Cecilia Bloomingdale (b. 1966). A budding journalist, Ann "reports" family events in a myriad of letters, diaries, and journals. (Try living with a teenager who takes notes!) She is already eligible for a Pulitzer, having accomplished what must be a "first" in writing history: last Christmas she wrote *two* thank-you notes to her grandmother.

Timothy Cooney Bloomingdale (b. 1967). Like his sister Peg, Tim matured early, like about two. Unlike his siblings, he never broke his toys, or lost his mittens, or aimed his baseballs at the kitchen window. In grade school he always did his assignments and never threw spitballs at the cute blonde in the front row. In junior high, however, he "regressed" into adolescence, screaming at his siblings, ignoring his parents and teachers, cooperating in every classroom caper, and finally achieving his ultimate goal: the attention of that cute blonde in the front row.

Patrick Templeton Bloomingdale (b. 1969). Being "the baby" of the family has not bothered Patrick a bit; in fact, he takes advantage of it. With complete self-confidence, he cons his big brothers into keeping him in sports equipment and loose change, and with a blarney worthy of his ancestors, he charms his sisters into helping him with his homework or taking his turn at the dishes. An ardent fan of the Nebraska Cornhuskers and the Oakland Raiders, Patrick is determined to make football his career. (With his slender build, he may never make a team, but with his big mouth, he might well replace Howard Cosell.)

Up a Family Tree is not an autobiography; it is merely the mad ramblings of a mother, telling tales about ten crazy kids, one nutty daughter-in-law, two perfect parents, four wonderful grandparents, ten aunts and uncles, cousins too numerous to mention, and two dumb dogs.

Most of the tales are true, but the facts and the names have been interchanged to protect the guilty.

UP A FAMILY
TREE

1

The Destroyers

Last Christmas Eve, as our family gathered around the tree for the traditional opening of the gifts, our grown son, John, received a calculator. As John unwrapped the package and removed the calculator from its box, his eye took on an old familiar gleam. He glanced at me, winked at his siblings, and with a mischievous grin said:

"Hey, this is neat. C'mon guys, let's take it apart and see how it works!"

For one awful moment I thought he meant it, for truly there had been many a Christmas when the gifts did not survive the day, so curious were our kids to "see how it works."

All of our children share one special talent: With little or no effort, and even less thought, they can break absolutely anything. No matter how well-made the item, or how long the guarantee, if it can be touched by human hands, it can be broken by a Bloomingdale . . . and given time, probably will be.

Our kids did not develop this talent overnight. In fact they did not develop it at all; they were born with it.

As young as six weeks of age, a Bloomingdale baby could yank the pin from his diaper, bend it beyond repair, and clutch it in his tiny fist until the opportunity arose to stab the hand that changed him.

At two months old, he could crack the sturdiest baby rattle, thus releasing the pebbles for more intriguing purposes, such as poking in an ear or stuffing up a nostril.

By six months of age, he could bounce a jumpseat until it fell apart, and lean out of a high chair until it toppled over.

Before he was strong enough to pull himself to his feet, our baby could pull the wheels off of toy trucks, or the stuffing out of animals. (Pooh-Bear and Piglet didn't mind, but the neighbor's cat did complain.) By his second birthday, he could take apart the baby's crib . . . with the baby still in it.

This did compound my problem, the fact that I had a new baby every year. And each seemed to be more destructive than his predecessor. By the time our first daughter was born I had a four-year-old hitting baseballs through the neighbor's windows, a three-year-old taking apart his brother's tricycle, a two-year-old flushing alphabet blocks down the toilet, and a one-year-old breaking out the bars of his playpen.

Our boys were so notorious for breaking things, a thoughtful neighbor named Mrs. Kelly once bought them a toy then new on the market: a Tonka truck. It was a marvelous toy for children, heavy steel, all one piece, with no moveable parts or jagged edges.

"I thought of your boys immediately when I saw this truck," said Mrs. Kelly proudly, "because it's guaranteed not to break."

And she was right; it didn't break. In fact, it didn't even dent when our three-year-old hit our two-year-old over the head with it. Of course the head broke, but then that wasn't guaranteed.

Our little sons became defensive about their notorious reputation, for they often got blamed for things they didn't do; and sometimes for things that weren't even done.

I remember on one occasion, shortly after our first daughter was born, I decided that her bathtime would be an ideal opportunity to explain to my toddler sons the "difference" of a sister. So I gathered them around the bath table and let them watch me undress the baby. As I took off her diaper, before I could say a word, our three-year-old took one look at his bare baby sister and cried:

"I didn't break it off, Mom! Honest! Mike musta did it!"

All of our children were intrigued by things electrical. They would plug in the iron "to see the pretty pattern it burns on the rug." They would get out the blender, and feed it candy, or gum, or popcorn. They would drop crayons into the toaster; toss socks into the ceiling vent of the attic fan; shoot water pistols into the back of the TV set. They blew so many fuses I stayed slim just running up and down the basement stairs.

This obsession with electricity drove my cleaning lady wild. Her name was Marguerite, and the only thing she feared more than electrical shocks were my children. But she was a very compassionate lady, and every week when she would come to clean, she would insist that I "get away for an hour or two; I'll watch the little monsters."

I remember on one such occasion (I don't remember the date, but I do remember that we then had seven children, the oldest eight years old), I decided to accept Marguerite's offer, and I went to the beauty salon to get my hair done. But it was a wasted trip, for I had no sooner walked into the shop than the electricity went off. The manager called the power company and discovered that it was not just a minor outage; in fact, the power was out in seven states. As there seemed little chance that it would be repaired soon, I turned around and went back home.

As I walked in the door, I found all the kids lined up in the living room, and Marguerite interrogating them: "Okay you guys," she said sternly, "I know one of you did it; better 'fess up, or I'll punish all of you!"

"Oh Marguerite," I interrupted with a laugh, "the electricity is not off just here at our house; it's out all over the midwest!"

"Oh, Lordy!" she groaned, "they really did it this time, didn't they? I'm sorry, Teresa; I tried to watch them, but they just got away from me!"

I never did convince her that the Bloomingdale boys were not responsible for the damage done at a dam in South Dakota; she would never believe that even such a vast distance could deter them.

Our children were always adept at taking things apart; unfortunately, they never developed a talent for putting things back together again. Thus, we would find in such unlikely places as the sandbox, the refrigerator, or the cabinet under the bathroom sink, such things as a piece of Dad's Pentax, or the top off his Parker pen, or an unidentifiable something that looked like it belonged on, or in, the telephone. We would consider ourselves lucky if we could then find the rest of the camera, the bottom of the pen, or the telephone, an instrument which, perhaps understandably, has always fascinated our kids.

As recently as last spring I came down to the kitchen and found my husband shouting into the telephone: "Well I can hear you, why can't you hear me?" Obviously, the phone was out of order.

"Call the phone company and get this repaired or replaced," he said, and I assured him I would. But first, out of habit I suppose, I unscrewed the mouthpiece of the phone and, sure enough, the speaker was missing. I found it, in a kitchen drawer, nestled among the knives and forks; how or why it got there I have no idea. And I never got around to interrogating anybody, because I was distracted by my husband, who was standing in the middle of the kitchen holding the oven door. He was looking dazed, because the oven door which he was holding was no longer attached to the oven.

"I just opened the oven to heat up the coffee cake," he said, "and the damn door fell off. I assume there is an explanation for this."

"Oh yeah," said our sixteen-year-old Peg, who had just come down to breakfast, "I forgot to tell you about that, Mom. When Martha was over here last night we got talking about ovens that have doors that can be removed for cleaning, and we decided to see if ours comes off. It does . . . sort of."

The "sort of" means that although the oven door does come off, it doesn't go back on again, at least not without $50 worth of aid from the appliance repair man.

Through the years our children have indulged in many idiocies, some of which I could understand (almost), but most of which remain a mystery.

For example, I could maybe understand how our nine-year-old John could climb out of our third-floor window, and lie on a nine-inch ledge 40 feet above the ground to paint, in huge black letters underneath the eaves of our newly painted white house: JOHN THE GREAT. But I could not understand why he took three-year-old Danny along to hold the paint.

I could understand how a seventeen-year-old girl could become so engrossed in a telephone conversation that she doesn't realize that she is absentmindedly picking at the wallpaper. What I could not understand was how she could peel off two panels of grasscloth without anybody interrupting her.

I could understand how a seven-year-old boy who had lost

his home in a tornado might hate his new house so much he
would burst into tears and scream: "I want to go home; I hate
this house!" I could even understand how he might become so
overwrought that he would kick a hole in his bedroom door.
But I could not understand why, after surveying the damage,
he then went across the hall and kicked a hole in his sister's
door. After all, *she* didn't cause the tornado. (At least nobody
ever proved it.)

I could understand how my children might break things ac-
cidentally, or absentmindedly, or inadvertently; I just could
never understand why they broke things on purpose, to "see
how it works." They take apart their watches, their radios,
their stereos, my car . . . just to see what makes them tick.

Our kitchen cabinets are filled with pieces and parts of
long-forgotten "projects" that somebody started, but never
finished. At least I think the pieces and parts are still in that
cabinet; I haven't been able to open it since Lee decided it
was "a little warped; let me fix it for you."

I would like to think that our kids have outgrown their reputation for breaking things, but somehow I doubt it. Just the
other day I saw my neighbor, Mary Jo, impulsively reach
for her newborn infant just because Patrick had peeked into
the crib and said: "Isn't he neat? Hey, Tim, look at the way
he folds his fingers up into his fist. I wonder how he does
that . . ."

2

Awful Aspects of a Big Family

In my book *I Should Have Seen It Coming When the Rabbit Died,* I devoted one chapter to the positive aspects of a big family: the fun, the laughter, the togetherness, the good times, et cetera.

Based on that one chapter alone, four thousand libraries catalogued my book under "fiction," sixty-two bookstores promoted it as "fantasy," thirteen reviewers commented on my "vivid imagination" and "creativity," and one critic in Connecticut told me to "take off those rose-colored glasses and tell it like it is." (There's one in every world; somebody always wants to point out the clouds drifting around my silver lining.)

I admit that there are negative aspects endemic to a big

family, but I didn't mention them in that book because I felt
that people who live in big families are all too familiar with
them, and the rest of you are better off not knowing.

Actually, there are some absolutely awful aspects about life
in a big family, and as I have misplaced my rose-colored spec-
tacles, I am now ready to admit to the worst of them.

1. *Money:* There is never enough of it. But this problem
is not limited to big families, as I have learned over the years.
Contrary to what my relatives believe, my husband and I did
not have all ten of these kids at the same time, or even two at
a time. Thus I can speak as an experienced parent of an "only
child," of two children, of three children, and on down the
line. Take it from me: no matter how few or how many children you have, or how little or how much money you make,
your expenses are going to exceed your income by approximately a hundred dollars a month. This is an economic fact of
life, so learn to live with it and take consolation in the knowledge that few parents end up in debtor's prison.

2. *Sleep:* Like money, sleep is most notable for its absence. But this cannot be blamed on the fact that there are too
many children; rather, there are too few parents. I have concluded that every family with more than two children needs
more than one mother. I realize that the modern father is very
good about assuming such traditional maternal chores as getting up in the middle of the night to feed the new baby, but
is the modern mother sleeping? No. She is lying awake waiting for the modern father to ask: "How do you heat the formula?" "How much is he supposed to drink?" "What do I do
if he spits up?" "YOU SAID HE WOULDN'T SPIT UP!"
In a big family, by the time the new baby has learned to sleep
through the night he is no longer the new baby. And when
the new New Baby awakes for that middle-of-the-night feed-

ing, Old Baby is bound to wake up and demand equal attention. So now neither parent gets any sleep, a trend which will continue throughout the next two decades when Mom walks the floor waiting for one or more teenagers to come home, and Dad lies awake feeling guilty because he is not walking the floor with Mom. You can see where an extra mother would come in handy. I once expressed that thought to my mother, who said: "Teresa, if there were two wives in your household, there would undoubtedly be twenty children."

As a singular wife who hasn't closed an eye since 1956, I strongly recommend that parents planning a big family forget about sleep.

3. *Clothes:* Buying clothes for this many kids is a minor irritant compared to the problem of keeping track of the clothes you have bought. It's impossible to remember what belongs to whom. I long ago gave up trying to identify such things as socks and underwear; we have a communal box for both, distinguished only by gender, and sometimes not even that. I turn a deaf ear to cries of "He's wearing my jeans!" and "Make her take off my blouse!" (The problem gets solved faster without me.) I have learned that little boys' shoes really do walk away all by themselves, and that socks thrown into a washing machine change color or size or just disappear. I have also learned a few tricks of the trade: If I buy an "on sale" shirt that is sure to fit Pat but which I know he will hate, I simply tell him I bought it for Tim. Tim won't want it, of course, since he thinks I bought it for him, but Pat, thinking it's Tim's, will spend the next six months "stealing" it. I have learned to buy "neuter" jackets . . . that is, no buttons, no pastels, no decals, no trim, just a plain sexless jacket for boys to hand down to girls or vice versa.

I have learned that a stray right-hand mitten, turned inside out, will fit a left hand and that on a bitter cold morning even a teenage boy will settle for mittens. My greatest coup was convincing a kindergartner that "Captain Kangaroo often wears one zippered boot with one buckled boot." (Forgive me, Captain, for the lies I have told in your name.)

4. *Placing the Blame:* Don't bother. Cornering a culprit, in a big family, is similar to picking up the mercury from a broken thermometer; it can't be done. Kids in a big family become experts at bouncing blame back and forth and betwixt and between until it gets lost in the shuffle or the offense is forgotten, whichever comes first. "Who left the bike in the driveway?" asks Dad. "It must have been Tim," says Peg. "It's his bike." "But you rode it last!" cries Tim, and Peg bounces back with: "No I didn't, Annie did." Ann grabs the blame and tosses it off with: "I put it away, but I saw Pat pushing it out of the garage," and Pat whacks back: "That's a lie; I wouldn't be caught dead on that dumb bike!" To which Tim replies: "If I ever catch you on that bike, you sure will be dead!" And on and on it goes till Dad is perfectly willing to forgive and forget if they would just SHUT UP!

5. *Questions:* Many children means many questions. Not necessarily many different questions. For example: "What's for dinner tonight, Mom?" when asked by seven children in four minutes is enough to make a mother sick of her own menu, if not her own children, especially when six of the seven react with: "Meat loaf again? Yecchhh!" In a big family, the anticipated questions about sex need only be answered once. From then on, the only question on that subject is: "Mom, that isn't true, is it?"

The most oft-repeated question in a big family is the same question that is most oft repeated in any family: "Can I borrow some money?" The only difference in a big family is the puzzle as to why that question should be so oft repeated when the answer is always "No."

6. *Transportation:* It is a big-family fact of life that when anybody has to be someplace at a given time, somebody else has to be someplace else at the same time. I have spent years trying to go in six different directions at once, constantly apologizing to children who will necessarily reach their destination too early or too late or sometimes not at all. Getting into a car pool is not the answer. When you have a big family, you *are* a car pool. For those of you who may be planning a big family, I suggest you buy a home near a bus line. Or better yet, buy the bus line; you'll use it a lot more than you do the home.

7. *Meal Planning:* Planning a meal for a big family is like placing the blame. It's impossible. If I cook dinner for twelve, three show up. If I am trying to stretch leftovers, all twelve show up, and six of them bring friends. In twenty-five years of motherhood I have never cooked a meal that came out even.

8. *Remembering:* While kids in a big family remember everything ("I don't suppose you'll come to my senior banquet, since you wouldn't even go to my kindergarten roundup!"), their parents never remember anything including the names of their kids. ("You. . . . Tim. . . . Pat. . . . Dan . . . whateveryournameis!") My son Tim told me recently that he doesn't mind so much if I call him Dan or Pat, but he would appreciate it if I would try not to call him Betsy. My explanation that Tim is the most congenial of my children, as my sister Betsy was the most congenial of my siblings, is not acceptable to Tim. (Though it is to Betsy, who has been known to call her wiseacre son Jim "Teresa.")

Some examples of "big-family forgetfulness": You tell six of the kids not to use the front door because the hinges are loose, but you forget to tell Number Seven, who walks in and the door falls off. Or you tell nine of the kids that you're

going to a late movie, but you neglect to mention it to the eldest (who, it goes without saying, does not communicate with
his siblings) and you come home to find the police filling out
a charge of child abandonment.

Last Saturday my husband yelled at Tim and Pat for playing on the front lawn where we had just laid new sod.

"I told you kids the last time we laid sod to stay off it!" he
exclaimed, and I had to remind him that the last time we laid
sod was fifteen years ago; sure he told somebody not to play
on the sod, but it couldn't have been Tim and Pat; they had
not yet been born.

9. *Space:* Like money, the supply never meets the demand. Over the years, as our children increased and multiplied and overflowed the bedrooms, I developed an obsession
about space. (Though not about money; I always trusted in
God to supply enough money, but I have never been sure
that Someone who exists in infinity could understand about
space.)

In the first ten years of our marriage, we moved so many
times my father accused us of trying to keep one step ahead of
the landlord. He was partly right. We were trying to keep
one step ahead of the Lord. Every time we would get settled
in a residence, the good Lord would send us another new
"resident" and we would have to start thinking about moving
again.

When we were expecting our fifth and last child (I know
now she wasn't our last child; I just didn't know it then), we
bought a four-bedroom house, which we thought would be
perfect for our family. Except it wasn't. The papers had been
signed and filed before we found out that the fourth bedroom
(a sun porch) was unheated and therefore unusable in winter. So our four-bedroom house was really a three-bedroom
house, which meant we had to double-bunk our four sons in

one bedroom, while their baby sister slept in the tiny nursery. Thirty months later, we had another baby.

For a while Danny shared the nursery with his sister, Mary, but the following year Peggy was born, so we had to move Danny's crib in with the double bunks. When the oxygen gave out, we moved eight-year-old Lee onto a hide-a-bed in the living room and sent a serious message to God on the subject of space. His answer? Annie.

Actually, we had decided to move before Annie came along. Our decision was prompted by a tiny sign posted on the little bunkside table where our seven-year-old son, John, kept all his treasures. The sign read:

"This is John's corner. Keep out."

So we moved into a huge house where John had his own room and a few years later into an even bigger split-level where he had his own level. Did that help? Of course not! He spent his entire high school career muttering, along with his siblings, "I need space, Man! Give me space!"

With four of our children now grown and gone, we have more than enough space for the family, and, in fact, we have tried to persuade our college-age kids to live at home until they marry. But they prefer to be "on their own," even if it means living in the "spacious quarters" of an overcrowded college dorm, a too-tiny apartment, or a tiered-bunk barracks. (Where they never, ever complain about space!)

And I think that's the most awful aspect of all. Not the children growing up and leaving home; that's to be expected. But they don't have to be so happy about it!

the baby we hadn't planned on having and whose sex we thought only God could determine. If we had had to decide whether to have a boy or a girl (or even if we had had to decide whether to have a baby at all), we probably would have remained childless forever.

If scientists are going to place such a burden of decision on young parents, I, as an old parent, feel compelled to comment on the subject, with which I am all too familiar.

As our sons outnumber our daughters by more than two to one (seven sons and three daughters), I am sometimes accused of favoring the girls, but this is not true. I don't love my sweet, beautiful daughters any more than I love their weird, goofy brothers. In fact, I have frequently wavered back and forth, in my prejudices and partialities, from girls to boys, daughters to sons. Thus, I feel qualified to offer an objective appraisal of all children, male and female.

It is an undisputed tradition that most new parents want to start their family with a son and heir. This is rather ridiculous for any number of reasons, not the least of which is: If you have any children at all, it is unlikely that you will ever accrue enough wealth for *anybody* to inherit. So forget about the heir, if not the son.

However, as a mother who gave birth to four sons before being blessed with a daughter, I would advise you, should the choice be yours, to start off with a girl . . . a strong, healthy lass who can someday serve a reasonable tenure as a baby sitter for her younger siblings.

On the other hand, starting off with a girl may brainwash you into believing that babies are so cute and sweet and adorable you would like to have a dozen of them, which is okay as long as you realize that if you have twelve kids the odds are that one or more of them is bound to be a boy.

Despite what you are thinking, I am not biased against boy babies. As a matter of fact, I consider boy babies much more

3

Sons vs. Daughters

I understand that medical scientists are now working on a project which will make it possible for would-be parents to predetermine the sex of the child they plan to procreate.

I can't imagine anything more mind boggling than weighing the pros and cons of boys and girls in an effort to decide whether to have a son or a daughter.

If young couples take this scientific project seriously, it just may mean the end of the human race. If would-be parents are going to sit around and argue "Let's have a little boy!" versus "But I want to have a little girl!" by the time they decide to have one or the other they may be too old to have either.

In the days when we were young and fruitful, my husband and I spent long, agonizing hours arguing over what to name exciting than girl babies, in that they are so much more unpredictable. One moment a baby boy will be sleeping soundly in his crib, and the next moment (when he realizes you have tiptoed out of the nursery, perhaps to catch a catnap on the sofa) he will be bashing his crib against the nursery wall, not so much to be naughty as to see if this dumb crib will collapse. (It will.)

Of course, if you start off with a boy, you do learn all the tricks of the trade fairly fast: how to corral the crib; how to secure a playpen (for heaven's sake, nail down that fold-up floor before he figures out how to unfold it and escape); where to buy washable, unbreakable, nonswallowable toys. Then, when you are finally blessed with a baby girl, she will be such a gentle joy you will hardly notice her tiny faults. (Alas, she, too, will leak and let you know about it, loudly, clearly, and frequently.)

There are other factors to be considered in choosing between a baby girl or a baby boy. Baby boys are cheaper. (Caution: This is not a continuing premise, so don't rush out and start a baby before you finish this book.)

While it is true that babies of either sex will require the same equipment: crib, bottles, playpen, high chair, et cetera, there will be a definite cost differential when it comes to clothes, though this may be your fault, rather than Baby's. For while mothers are seldom tempted to "dress up" a baby boy (anything warm and washable will do), a daughter is different. No mother can resist dressing her daughter in the manner in which her dolls were dressed two decades before. Dresses with frills, booties with bows or little bells, tiny socks with lace ruffles, embroidered petticoats. Why, it costs almost as much to dress a daughter as it did to dress your Barbie doll!

If babies were born in the toddler stage, there would be no problem at all about sex preference, for no parents in their right minds would choose a two-year-old boy over a two-year-old girl. (A decade later this decision will be completely reversed.) Fortunately, by the time your son is two years old, you have become somewhat attached to him and aren't too tempted to give him back. (Anyway, his warranty has run out.)

While a two-year-old girl will play quietly with her dolls, have a pretend tea party, or happily help Mommy with the housework, a two-year-old boy will more likely be outside tearing up the neighbor's tulips, taking apart his own tricycle, or trying to throw a baseball as far as your living-room window. However, even with mud under his fingernails, bubble-gum in his hair, and athletic abilities which cause a constant rise in your insurance premiums, a two-year-old boy may be more appealing than a two-year-old girl, especially if he is yours. Two-year-old boys, even at their worst (and they usually are), have a way of winning Mommy's heart, which may explain why, when people talk about "the terrible twos," Mommy can't seem to remember why they were so terrible.

Throughout the next few years, the balance of prejudice continues to favor the girls. Come kindergarten time, little girls are definitely more sophisticated than little boys. While a five-year-old boy is still clutching his mother's knees and wailing: "I wanna go home!" a five-year-old girl will have already introduced herself to the teacher, the principal, and the play-ground monitors, taken charge of the chalk board, and appointed herself paper passer-outer.

This maturity continues throughout most of grade school, where girls are smarter, quicker, and, let's face it, just plain gooder. They seldom get called to the principal's office to explain how the thumbtacks got on the teacher's chair or the garter snake got into the girls' lavatory. They can be counted on to deliver messages between teacher and parents, to show up on time for glee club, choir, or play practice, and they never disrupt the class by throwing spitballs, shooting rubber bands, or making noises which they hope will sound obscene.

Of course, some parents, as well as some teachers, may prefer the challenge of matching wits with a ten-year-old boy. I, myself, have been accused of such preferences, usually by goody-goody girls who won't find the answer to "How can you possibly love a kid like that?" until they have an impish little Puck of their own.

By junior-high-school age, the balance of prejudice suddenly plunges on the side of the boys, for as no mother in her right mind would opt for a two-year-old boy over a two-year-old girl, neither would that same mother (presuming she is still sane by this time) prefer a thirteen-year-old girl over her male counterpart.

Somewhere around the age of twelve or thirteen, the little lad who has spent a dozen years driving his mother wild will suddenly become loving and helpful, kind and courteous. There is no reasonable explanation for this phenomenon; it may just be nature's way of balancing the sexual scales, for it is at this very age that Mommy's Sweetheart, the darling daughter who has never given a moment's concern, suddenly becomes stubborn, rebellious, self-righteous, and bossy.

If a woman is ever elected President of the United States, I hope we have the good sense to elect a girl who is in the early stages of adolescence. And I have just the girl for the job. Our daughter Annie has an answer for every question, a solution for every problem. Of course, most of them don't make any sense, but that has never daunted Annie, and certainly such total self-confidence is important in a leader. Actually, some of her ideas sound pretty practical to me. For example, when the Panama Canal issue was raised in 1979, Annie had what I thought was the perfect solution:

"Give it back to them just the way we found it . . . filled with dirt."

If our Annie were President, the continuing crises in the Middle East would certainly come to an end. Annie would not have to threaten sending in the Marines, or enforcing embargoes, or even using nuclear weapons. All she would have to suggest would be a state visit. After being subjected to Annie for a week or so, even the most determined terrorists would capitulate.

It is true that thirteen- and fourteen-year-old girls complain a lot, but maybe they have reason to. As a mother who has watched three daughters endure that awful period of adolescence, I am aware of the fact that for them, at that age, everything in their lives is out of whack. While a teenage girl's face is breaking out, the rest of her is refusing to fill out, and, as a consequence, her clothes, whatever the size, never fit. She is too big for children's clothes, but still too little for teen fashions. Everything she tries on is either too short or too long, too "sweet" or too sophisticated. Shopping with her is a hopeless venture, for in the unlikely event that you do find an ensemble that fits her awkward form, you can be sure she won't like it.

In fact, she won't like anything . . . not her clothes, her school, her family, or her life. Her friends are suddenly all "fickle," her siblings "impossible," her parents and teachers equally "out-of-it." Her total vocabulary consists of three sentences: "It's not my turn!" "How come you never yell at *him?*" and *"Nothing's* the matter!"

A thirteen-year-old boy, on the other hand, is just the opposite. His friends have become indispensable to him; his parents have become not only tolerable but sometimes even likeable; even school has become almost interesting.

If there is a single comparison to be made between a thirteen-year-old boy and a thirteen-year-old girl, it is: at this age, his mind begins to open, while hers definitely slams shut.

However, the balance of prejudice reverses in her favor at

age sixteen, when, for reasons unknown to most civilized adults, adolescents of both sexes are given a license to drive.

Despite the fact that a sixteen-year-old girl has a closed mind and a big mouth, she has one important point in her favor: she won't raise your auto-insurance rates, as will a sixteen-year-old boy. As a parent who had four sons simultaneously striving to make us insurance-poor, I may be overly sensitive on the subject. I will not bore you with our family financial statistics covering fender-benders, traffic violations, incredible mileage (Did you know that it takes twelve gallons of gasoline to drive to the library and back? Ten blocks?!), and just plain carelessness. (Has anybody seen the knob to the car radio? The cigarette lighter? The back-seat floor mats? The license plates?) Suffice it to say that, at this age, I tend to be partial to daughters.

Teenage girls cost less than teenage boys not just in the car, but also in the kitchen, for while a seventeen-year-old girl subsists almost entirely on cinnamon tea and unbuttered toast, a seventeen-year-old boy needs six huge meals a day and at least that many snacks.

However, while daughters may be cheaper to transport and feed, there is economic chaos in their closets, which are stuffed with clothes they "cannot possibly be expected to wear." While your teenage son will wear the same sweater and blue jeans day and night throughout the entire school year, your daughter dare not be seen wearing the same outfit twice.

As one who has been dodging debtor's prison by juggling the credit cards of various clothing stores, I offer one important piece of advice to parents of growing children. Make your teenagers get after-school (or at least summertime) jobs so they can pay for their own clothes, car expenses, entertainment, and traffic fines, because you are going to need every dollar *you* make to send them to college.

And that's an even more important bit of advice: send them to college. I mean *away* to college. I don't care if you live in Cambridge, New Haven, Palo Alto, or South Bend, don't take advantage of your hometown academics. You simply can't afford it. The food he steals from your refrigerator and the clothes she stores in her closet will cost much more than tuition, dorm fees, books, and even "essentials" in an away-from-home college.

Like where? Have you considered, perhaps, the University of Pago-Pago?

4

Minding the Money

"What's the matter with you?" I asked my young friend Diane, the other day, and she wailed:

"My husband took my checkbook and credit cards away from me!"

"Congratulations!" I shouted cheerfully before she continued with the expected explanation: she was spending too much money; she couldn't balance her checkbook; she couldn't keep track of her credit-card charges . . . every housewife knows the story.

"But how could this happen?" cried Diane. "My husband isn't a hidebound chauvinist; he's all for women's liberation, equal rights, equal responsibilities, the whole bit!"

"Don't worry about it, Diane," I counseled from my years

of juggling debits, overdrafts, and a frugal spouse. "It won't last."

"What do you mean, 'it won't last'?" she asked.

"Give your husband six months of battling the banks and arguing with computers, and I guarantee he'll toss the whole mess back to you, though I don't know why you'd want it. Frankly, I've always envied those housewives who had to "make do" on a simple allowance while their husbands paid all the bills and did all the accounting."

How did we housewives fall into the bookkeeping business, anyway? Since when did paying the bills, balancing the budget, robbing Peter to pay Paul, and hiding the overdrafts become our job? How did this traditionally husband's role become the wife's responsibility?

I don't know if mine is a typical female reaction, but I am allergic to money. I break out in a cold sweat when I spend it, and I get sick to my stomach when I must account for it. I even hate the sight of it; last month I found a five-dollar bill tucked away in a summer purse, and it caused a domestic crisis. My son claimed it was his. (How, then, did it get into *my* purse?) My daughter said it must be hers, as she had borrowed the purse last August, and she was "almost sure" she had left some money in it. On hearing about it, my husband "suddenly remembered" that I owed him five dollars, but before any of us could settle the matter, the purse got "misplaced" and when it was finally found, the five-dollar bill was (you guessed!) gone. Since we didn't know which kid took it, we had to punish all of them and thus live with cries of "No fair!" "Unjust!" and "My brothers and sisters are thieves and liars!" You can understand why I hate money.

Don't misunderstand me. I don't hate *wealth*. (How could I? I've never even met it, let alone lived with it.) No, its not luxury living I hate; it's that "filthy lucre," the "coin of the realm," those nickels, dimes, and dollars that are so difficult to accumulate, so hard to hold on to, and so impossible to account for!

Money has been complicating my life since my fourth birthday when my father gave me a shiny new Jefferson nickel, and I didn't know what to do with it. Oh, I knew what it was worth: five gumballs, or a candy bar, or a bottle of soda pop. But I was terribly frustrated because, while I was suddenly affluent, I was also "confined to quarters." Few four-year-olds are allowed to toddle off down to the candy store.

So, after careful consideration, I did the only thing feasible. I entrusted my nickel to the kid next door—who, being a sophisticated seven-year-old, was allowed to venture the two blocks to the candy store—and asked him to buy me a candy bar. Needless to say, I never saw the nickel again, nor the candy bar, and the kid conveniently "forgot" the entire transaction, though he returned from the store with chocolate all over his face.

To make matters worse, that evening my father asked me what I had done with my nickel, and thus began a lifetime of explaining to the man-in-my-life just how, why, and where I had squandered his money.

Admittedly, for the next few years I didn't have that problem, for during grade school and high school I blithely sponged off my parents, accepting both the necessities and the luxuries in life as my due, and accounting for my weekly allowance with the same excuse kids have been using for centuries: "I spent it all on school supplies."

It was at age eighteen that I fell into that financial whirlpool that has trapped so many economic innocents over the years: I opened my first checking account.

Checking accounts are diabolical inventions created, supposedly, to keep us from soiling our hands with that "filthy lucre." We deposit our paychecks in the bank, pay for our purchases by check, and never need to touch all those dirty old dimes and dollars.

What they don't tell you, when you open a checking account, is that while it is true you will never again have to handle money, it is also true that you will never again know exactly how much money you have, though you can be sure that it is less than you think you have.

There are two pertinent points everyone should remember when dealing with a bank.

1. When you make a deposit, you must allow at least five days for the money to travel from the teller's window across the room to the bookkeeper's desk, and another two or three days for the computer to accredit your account.

2. On the other hand, when you write a check, you must assume that it will travel through the teller, the bookkeeper, the computer, and your account in approximately seventeen seconds.

This will explain why a check written at noon on July fifth may bounce by 12:03 (and word of said transaction will reach your husband at the restaurant where he is having lunch). Your argument that you deposited a zillion dollars on July first will not clear you with the bank, your husband, or more important, the computer, which won't notify *you* of any overdrafts until a week after they go through, by which time you will have written several more "bad" checks for which you will be dunned $7.00 each by the bank. (You didn't think they were in this business for fun, did you?)

To avoid overdrafts, bounced checks, and the service charges accompanying either or both, you are advised to record, in your check-sized record book, the date, amount, payee, and purpose of every check you write, as well as the balance then remaining in your account.

This little record book, which the bank gives you free along with your checks (which are *not* free, but that's a whole new chapter), is very handy for jotting down telephone numbers, making grocery lists, or keeping memos of things you were supposed to do last Thursday. However, it is useless as a check record, because no matter how faithfully you record your checks, or how carefully you subtract the amount of each check, your balance will never, ever coincide with the balance shown on your end-of-the-month bank statement, which will be sent to you in the middle of next month, by which time you will have written twenty-three more checks that have not yet had a chance to go through.

Thus, to find out how much money you actually do have in the bank, you must spend the remainder of the afternoon (or if you are in the muddle I'm in, the remainder of the week) checking off your canceled checks, adding up your outstanding checks, subtracting same from your statement's balance, and cursing wildly because it is always less than the balance in your checkbook.

Some months the difference may be as much as a hundred dollars; more often it will be a frustrating amount, like thirty-seven cents, which leaves you in a real dilemma. Is it worth spending an entire afternoon trying to find thirty-seven cents?

Not to me, it isn't. So to balance my own checkbook each month, I simply record whatever is necessary in the following manner: "37 cents to cover embezzlement by somebody at the bank."

If you think a bank statement is confusing, however, just compare it to a credit-card statement. I am not referring here to in-store accounts, where your neighborhood department store sends you a statement clearly noting that your son Dan signed a charge slip for three rock albums in the music department on the eighth of August. With that nice clear statement, you not only know which kid to kill but also what merchandise to return, and where.

I am referring, instead, to those bank credit cards (you might have known the bank would be involved) that indicate only that invoice #79203 was purchased at store #67 in department #86 by an unknown person using your credit card. (An illegible code on the back of the bill supposedly interprets their number system, but nobody has ever been able to read it.)

Thus, you have no way of knowing which member of your family (and you can only trust that it was a member of your family) purchased what, where, or even for how much, because by the time the postal service (and that's a whole new book!) gets the bill to you, an 18 percent finance charge has been added. (Note: Don't ever, ever try to figure out how or on what they compute that 18 percent; you have neither the time, nor the patience, to fight that battle. Just resign yourself to it; like death and taxes, it's inevitable.)

I have resolved again and again to stop using bank credit cards, but just as I am allergic to money, so am I addicted to credit cards. They are far too convenient to use: no dirty old dimes and dollars to handle; no immediate reckoning . . . and with any luck, I'll drop dead before the first of the month when I have to explain the whole mess to my spouse.

Periodically, I tear up all my credit cards (or more often, the banks request that I tear up my credit cards) and determine never again to charge anything, anywhere, anytime. But after a month or two, the bank misses me and begins to woo me with love letters tempting me to "buy now, pay later," and as by this time I am sick to death of trying to keep track of the cash in my purse (or of trying to track down the kid who absconded with said cash), I fill out the attached application and start all over again.

In twenty-five years of juggling a household budget, I

admit that I have never balanced my checkbook or received a credit-card statement saying: "Nothing due." My husband doesn't approve of this, of course, but he learned long ago not to hassle me about my bookkeeping habits. He tried that once, in the early years of our marriage, and I tossed the checkbook, bills, and credit cards into his lap and said: "Here; you handle all the money and all the horrors that go with it. All I want is a five-dollar-a-week allowance."

Three months and sixteen overdrafts later he threw the whole mess back at me. It served me right for being so greedy; what did I want five dollars a week for? With three toddlers underfoot, I was once again "confined to quarters" and never got a chance to spend it.

I do envy Diane her money-free months, though I did warn her that they won't last. But in her case, maybe they will. After all, she is a young, liberated housewife, and as a strong-minded feminist, she just might be able to con her husband into controlling the money forever!

5

Kids Prepare for the Coming Hard Times

My frustrations concerning my own finances are nothing compared to the hair-tearing I have done over what has to be the greatest rip-off in economic history: children's allowances.

I don't know what idiot instigated the idea that kids should be financially independent, but I hope he will be forced to spend a suitable length of time in purgatory trying to come up with enough nickels, dimes, and quarters to keep an eight-year-old in ice cream cones, an eleven-year-old in school supplies, and a teenager in the lap of luxury.

When my husband and I started our family, we agreed that we would not follow the example of our older friends, who seemed to be paying their children to perform such herculean tasks as breathing, eating, and arguing. We determined that if our kids wanted spending money, they would have to earn it by helping with the household chores, taking care of the yard, washing our car, et cetera. We intended to pay them by the job, not by the hour. (Children can make a fortune in dawdling.) Thus, any child with enough initiative could earn money for movies, treats, or tennis lessons, while his lazy-loafer brother would get nothing more than meals.

Unfortunately, we got off to a bad start. Our first four sons were *all* lazy loafers.

I realize that toddlers aged one, two, three, and four are not ordinarily expected to work around the house, but a household with four kids under the age of five could hardly be considered ordinary. If their mother was going to survive, those kids, despite their tender years, would have to help, even if it meant doing nothing more than picking up toys, emptying wastebaskets, or scooting under the sofa to retrieve the baby's shoes, the baby's rattle, or, not infrequently, the baby. (If you were nine months old and crawling frantically among and between the flying feet of a roomful of brothers, you'd seek refuge under the sofa, too.)

However, our sons could not be tempted with promises of: "Help Mama fold the diapers and she'll buy you treats from the ice cream man," for our toddlers were, unfortunately, all men of independent means.

I don't mean to infer that they each had a private income from a family trust (to be honest with you, I don't even know what a family trust is), but what they did have were grand-parents who were suckers for a smile, a hug, and a tiny, out-stretched palm.

My in-laws, being typical grandparents, never came to visit empty-handed. They always brought a present for the baby, a tradition that evolved into a present for the baby and a toy for each of the toddlers.

After we had had four babies in four years, the toys began to accumulate to the point of absurdity, so Grandma bought each of the boys a piggy bank and told them she would give each of them a quarter every time she came to see them, and "before you know it, you'll have enough money to buy a bicycle." On each visit much ceremony was made of dropping the quarter into the piggy banks, which the boys would rattle enthusiastically to assure their grandparents that the money was still there.

Thus did my sons learn at a very early age three important facts of life: (1) it is indeed possible, if one plays his cards right, to get paid for doing nothing; (2) if one is industrious enough and patient enough, one can fish a quarter out of the slimmest piggy-bank slot; and (3) when rattled, a piggy bank full of pennies sounds amazingly similar to a piggy bank full of quarters.

By the time those four had reached school age, their grandmother had gone to God, their grandfather had gone into retirement, and the quarters had just gone. What had not gone was their continuing need for money. There were school supplies, scout expenses, candy treats, bubble gum and baseball cards, and no money to pay for them. I didn't mind subsidizing them so much as I minded keeping the accounting: to whom did I give how much for what?

So my husband and I decided to rethink our theories on allowances; perhaps it would, after all, be better to give them a set allowance and teach them how to live within their means.

How do you set an allowance for kids of varying ages? We tried the traditional chronological approach: a dime a week for each year of a child's age, but that proved impractical. A four-year-old certainly doesn't need forty cents a week, and a fourteen-year-old couldn't buy his way into half a movie for

$1.40. So we did what budget-makers have been doing for centuries: we robbed from Peter to pay Paul. The preschoolers and primary-grade kids got nothing; the middle schoolers got a buck a week, and the junior high kids, three dollars a week. At the age of fifteen the kids were told to "get a job" as there wasn't enough money in our budget (or for that matter, the national treasury) to subsidize the activities of our teenagers.

Once the question of "how much?" was settled, we had to tackle the question: "What for?" What would the kids be expected to pay for out of their allowances or salaries from after-school jobs, and what could they count on us, their parents, to pay for?

"This is how we shall determine who pays for what," said their father. "We'll separate everything into necessities and luxuries. Your mother and I will pay for necessities, such as school lunches, scout dues, athletic activities, and other school-related events, and you will pay for luxuries such as ice cream, candy, movies, rock records, posters, and library fines."

"Library fines?" asked Tim. "Since when are library fines a luxury?"

"Since when are they a necessity?" asked his dad. "If you have to pay those fines out of your allowance, maybe you'll learn to return your library books on time."

"Are you telling us that *everything* must be classified as either a luxury or a necessity?" asked Peg. "What would you consider shoes?"

"Shoes are a necessity, of course," said her father. "I'll buy your shoes."

"Good," said Peggy. "I need a pair of baby-blue ballet slippers for Laurie's costume party. They're seventeen dollars plus tax. Can I get them today?"

"Wait a minute!" said Dan. "I just bought a new pair of track shoes which I paid for with my own money. If you're gonna pay for Peg's ballet shoes, Dad, how about reimbursing me for those track shoes?"

"All right," sighed his father. "I suppose track is a school-related event. How much do I owe you?"

"Fifty-four dollars," said Dan.

"Fifty-four dollars!" moaned his father. "Where are you running? In the Olympics? Better you should have gone out for ballet!"

"Daddy," ventured Tim shyly, "if you're gonna pay for school-related events, will you pay for my fine at school?"

"Fine?" asked his father. "What fine?"

"Oh, the dumb teacher fined me twenty-five cents 'cause I threw a snowball at Jenny Morris, a new girl in our class."

"Shame on you, Tim," scolded his father, "and no, I will not pay your fine."

"But, Dad," argued our Tim, "you did say that if we paid for the luxuries, you'd pay for the necessities."

"That's right, I did," agreed his father. "But I hardly consider throwing a snowball at Jenny Morris a necessity."

"Oh, but it was, Dad," said Tim sincerely. "You see, if I didn't come up with ten cents before three o'clock I was gonna have to stay after school, and I couldn't stay after school because I had soccer practice, so it was absolutely necessary for me to get that dime—"

"You've lost me, Tim," interrupted his father. "What did you need the ten cents for?"

"Yesterday's fine," admitted Tim. "I got caught chewing gum, and the teacher said I had to bring a dime today *or else.*"

"But what's all this got to do with throwing a snowball at Jenny Morris?" asked his father.

"Well see, Dad, I bet Doug a dime that I could get Jenny Morris to talk to me, I mean to say more than just "Hi," and Doug bet I couldn't. So I threw a snowball at Jenny and she

turned around and said, 'Tim Bloomingdale, you cut that
out!' Doug paid me the dime, but the teacher fined me another twenty-five cents."

"Tell me, Tim," mused his father. "Did you enjoy it when
Jenny spoke to you?"

"You bet!" said Tim. "Jenny's the cutest girl in school!"

"Well, then," said his father judiciously, "that would class
the entire episode as a luxury, I think. Sorry, Tim; better luck
next time."

Sometime later we again got in the luxury *vs.* necessity
hassle when our seventeen-year-old son, Dan, came to me and
said:

"Mom, the prom's next week, and I'd sure like to go, but
I'm trying to save my job earnings for more important things.
You wouldn't consider giving me the money for the prom,
would you?"

I am a sucker for sentiment, and in my book the senior
prom is about the most sentimental event in one's high school
career. I wanted Dan to enjoy this "once in a lifetime" event,
and I understood his unwillingness to delve into his college
savings.

"Well, Dan," I said, "how much do you think it will cost?"

"I've got it all figured out," said Dan. "The whole evening
will cost just a little over a hundred dollars."

"A hundred dollars!" I cried. "That's insane! How could it
possibly cost that much to take a girl to a dance?"

"The tux rental alone will cost me thirty dollars," said Dan,
"then there are the shoes, spats, top hat, cane—"

"Hold it!" I said. "The tux I'll agree to; I'll even consent to
the formal shoes, considering the fact that you don't have anything else except those ratty tennis shoes, which, I have no
doubt, you would gladly wear with a tux, but I'm not paying
for spats, top hat, and cane."

"Okay," relented Dan, "so that's thirty-four dollars for tux and shoes. Then I'll need another twenty-five dollars for flowers for my date. . . ."

"Twenty-five dollars for flowers?" I wailed. "What are you buying her, a bridal bouquet? How about a nice five-dollar corsage?"

"Aw, Mom, corsages are so *common;* I thought a dozen long-stemmed roses would be more impressive."

"If you're paying for it, you can be impressive," I told him. "If I'm paying for it we'll be common. I'll compromise: ten dollars for a corsage. That's forty-four dollars, and another five for the prom ticket; you should get by with just under fifty."

"You forgot the banquet," said Dan. "The guys made reservations at that new French restaurant, and the dinner will cost thirty dollars a couple."

"Whatever happened to your addiction to the Golden Arches?" I asked sarcastically.

"Oh, that's where the breakfast will be," said Dan. "The guys are renting the whole place; the manager has agreed to decorate it, provide live music, and serve a special menu for just ten dollars a couple."

"Okay, okay," I sighed before he made the same suggestion his older brother had made several years before: to have the breakfast at our house. I know for a fact, you can't feed high school seniors a post-prom breakfast for ten dollars a couple. "But that only adds up to eighty-nine. I thought you said it would be over a hundred dollars?"

"Yeah," he said. "There's another twenty for the limousine."

I just looked at him. "You're joking, aren't you, Dan?"

"Joking?" he asked suddenly alert. "What do you mean?"

"You really don't plan on renting a limousine," I said, "do you?"

"Okay," he conceded graciously. "No limo. But how about

the other stuff? Can you afford to give me the eighty-nine dollars?"

"Of course I can't afford it," I said, "and of course I'll come up with the money somehow. After all, this is your only prom."

So I checked my bank account, cringed at the balance, and realizing that a check for eighty-nine dollars would throw my banker into apoplexy, I went to the Savings and Loan and withdrew the money from my Christmas Club account.

"Here you are, Dan," I said. "Enjoy the prom. By the way, who are you taking?"

"Oh, I'm not going to the prom," said Dan as he quickly pocketed the cash. "I just figured I was entitled to the money it would cost if I did go to the prom."

"But, Dan," I cried. "You lied to me!"

"No I didn't, Mom," he said. "If you recall our conversation, I said: "I would like to go to the prom." And I *would* like to go, but not bad enough to blow eighty-nine bucks on it. I'm gonna use this money for that weekend in Kansas City I told you about; a bunch of us are going to the baseball game."

"Dan, we discussed that some time ago, and I told you we can't afford to send you on that weekend trip."

"How can you say you can't afford it? You can afford to send me to the prom; why can't you afford the Kansas City trip?" Dan said, all too logically. "I don't see what difference it makes whether I go to a dance or a baseball game; it's all gonna cost the same."

Am I mistaken, or did I just pay a kid for arguing?

6

Methought I heard a voice cry: "SLEEP NO MORE!"

—Macbeth; II, ii, 36

When I was a little child my parents told me that God made night different from day in the hopes that human beings would catch on to the idea that we are supposed to sleep during the night and work during the day. And do you know, I believed them? I went to bed every single night and got up every single morning until it finally got to be a habit . . . one which, unfortunately, was impossible to sustain when I became a mother.

Recently I tried to explain this night-and-day theory to my

own children, and as I expounded the positive aspects of "getting a good night's sleep" they all looked at me like I was crazy. Maybe I was. It was two in the morning and at that hour I am not too bright.

I had gone to bed at 11 P.M. (old habits die hard) and had spent the next three hours answering questions:

"Mom, I hate to wake you, but have you seen my letter sweater? I need it for the pep rally tomorrow."

"Ma, I forgot to tell you; I got a three-day suspension for allegedly smoking in the locker room, so let me sleep late in the morning, okay?"

"Mother! Jim's on the phone. Will you accept the charges?"

"As long as you're up, Mom, do you want some pizza? We sent out for some!"

Doesn't anybody go to bed anymore? Or is it just my kids who stay up all night?

I should have realized my children would all be nocturnal, because from the day they were born they ran the clock backward. I would bring the newborn baby home from the hospital, place him gently in his crib, and he would sleep like a log . . . until 11 P.M. at which moment he would awake and want to visit, all night long. I spent half a lifetime rocking babies all night and poking them all day, but it never did any good. The longer I rocked, the louder they wailed; and the harder I poked, the sounder they slept.

By the time they got to be toddlers they understood that they had to go to bed at night, but by golly they weren't about to go to sleep! For that matter, they weren't about to stay in bed. They would pop up periodically, begging for a drink of water, another bedtime story, one more kiss, or Daddy to come kill the monster in the closet. I assume they eventually went to sleep, but I have never been positive of that fact, for by the time I would finally konk out they would still be whispering and giggling, and when I would awake, they would already be up, laughing and shouting and dismantling their bedroom.

Their ability to pop out of bed at the crack of dawn ended abruptly on the second day of school, from thenceforth it was not only a battle to get them to bed at night, but another battle to get them up in the morning.

My six-year-old son once asked me: "Why do little kids have to go to bed when they're not tired and get up when they are?"

I never knew the answer to that question, which seems strange after all the years I have argued about bedtime.

"Nine o'clock!" I used to announce each evening to my younger children. "Time for bed!"

"Aw, Mom, nine is a baby bedtime!" they would wail in protest. (Nonsense; baby doesn't go to bed till 5 A.M.) "Why can't we stay up till nine-thirty?"

"Because your big sister goes to bed at nine-thirty," I would explain with a logic only a mother of a large family can comprehend, "and if you stay up till then she'll want to stay up till ten, which she can't do because that's her older brother's bedtime, and he would then want to stay up till ten-thirty . . . and why am I arguing with you? GO TO BED!"

By the time my older kids got to be teenagers I gave up on them; I couldn't waste my energy forcing them to go to bed at night because I knew I would need it to get them up in the morning.

But it's college-age kids who really confound me. As far as I can figure, college kids never go to bed at all. When I finally shoo the last of my school-age youngsters off to bed at night, my college kids are just beginning to do their studying, having spent the early part of the evening involved in more important activities, such as washing their hair, raiding the refrigerator, and talking on the telephone. (Though how they ever get it away from Annie is beyond me.)

When I come down to the kitchen in the morning, they are still at the breakfast table, bent over their books, slurping cold coffee, and mumbling: "Only five thousand words to go; this paper's due by eight."

On the weekends, if I am tactless enough to suggest to my older children that perhaps they should stay home for a change and catch up on their sleep, they exclaim:

"Are you kidding? I haven't got time to sleep! I've got a big date (or a big game, or a debate tournament, or play rehearsal). Don't wait up for me tonight, because I don't know what time I'll be in!"

Well I know what time they'll be in; they'll be in by curfew or I'll know the reason why!

As a matter of fact, I spend the wee hours of most weekend mornings listening to the "reasons why" one or the other of my kids has not made it home by curfew.

Ours is a reasonable curfew: 11 P.M. for high school freshmen and sophomores; midnight for juniors and seniors; 1 A.M. for college age.

When our now-adult sons were teenagers, they were notorious about being late, but when they finally did come in, they always had some simple, sensible excuse like: "I wrecked the car" or "I got arrested and had to talk my way out of jail." By the time we had ascertained that the car wasn't actually wrecked, merely scratched (and wasn't that scratch there before?), or the speeder was not really arrested but merely given a warning and sent on his way, we were so relieved we forgot about the curfew.

But our fifth child, Mary, is nothing at all like her brothers. She is a much better driver than they (she doesn't even know where the traffic court is located; they could find it blindfolded, which is the way the traffic judge thinks they drive), but she is not nearly as creative. When she misses a curfew, she can never come up with anything more interesting than: "I couldn't find my car keys."

Just the other night the phone rang about midnight, and it was Mary, calling from the University of Nebraska at Omaha campus, where she had been rehearsing for the college play, another of her beloved Shakespearean dramas.

"I hope I didn't wake you, Mother," she said, knowing full well that I never close an eye till she is home, "but I thought I'd better call you and tell you that I may be a little late. In fact, you or Dad may have to come and get me."

"Don't tell me," I said with a sigh; "let me guess. You lost your car keys."

"They aren't *lost*, Mother," she said patiently. "They are merely *misplaced*. I'm almost positive I left them in the costume room."

"Why don't you go in the costume room and look, Mary?" I suggested sweetly.

"The costume room is locked," she said, "but I've called the security guard and he's going to come down and let me in so I can look for them."

"Well call me back if you can't find them," I told her, "and I'll have Dad bring you the other set of keys."

"Uhhhh . . . that may present a little problem, Mom," she said. "The keys I used tonight were the other set; I lost my keys last weekend. I meant to replace them, honest, but I just didn't have time! Don't panic. I'll pay for having another set made if I can't find these. But I'm sure they're in the costume room; here comes the guard now. See you!"

"Call me!" I said into a dead telephone. I hung up and began my Weekend Watch . . . watching the clock, watching for Mary, watching my husband to see if he would wake up and share all this fun.

By twelve-thirty Mary had neither come home nor called, so I phoned the security office at UNO.

"Mary Bloomingdale?" asked the guard cheerfully. "Sure, I know her. She's the student who can't keep track of her car keys. I just this minute left her."

"Is she on her way home?" I asked. "Did she find her keys?"

"Not this time," he said apologetically. "I feel bad about that, too. I've got almost a perfect record for finding Mary's car keys."

"Where is Mary now?" I asked. "Is she with you?"

"No," he said. "The last I saw of her she was walking toward the university parking lot. I figured she must know where she's going."

I don't know why he figured that; he may know a lot about Mary's keys, but he doesn't know much about Mary.

As I hung up the telephone, my husband woke up and I had to tell him that it was past midnight, and his daughter was out wandering around the university campus all by herself and didn't have any way of getting home because she had lost the car keys.

As he dragged himself wearily out of bed, I handed him a shoebox and said:

"Here. Sort through these; there ought to be a GM key in that lot someplace. Maybe it will fit our station wagon."

"What are you going to do?" he asked.

"What I do best," I said. "Worry."

As the minutes went by and we heard nothing from Mary, my husband tried to lighten my worries by making humorous comments about the key box.

"Ah, here's the key to Grandpa's Buick; sure glad you kept that, we can use it if the Buick is ever resurrected from the junkyard. Hey, wake Patrick and tell him I finally found his roller-skate key! . . . and what's this? A motel key. Are you saving this for any specific purpose? A rendezvous? A memento?"

"A mistake!" I said. "I carried that away from that motel we stayed at in the Ozarks. It was just a mistake."

"It certainly was!" he shuddered as he recalled that awful motel. It was so old I am surprised it even had a key.

"I don't believe it!" he crowed. "A key to the station wagon! C'mon, let's drive over to the university and see if we can find the car."

"We have to wait till we hear from Mary!" I said, nearing the panic point. "Where could she be? It's been almost an hour since she called!"

At that moment, the door opened and Mary breezed in with a cheerful:

"Hi! You guys still up? Sorry about the car keys—"

"Where have you been?" I interrupted.

"At Perkins'," she said innocently. "Cindy gave me a ride home, and since I still had half an hour before curfew, we stopped for a cup of coffee. You weren't worried, were you?"

Who, me? Worried? With so much worry, the least she could have done was wreck the car. I do so hate to waste good worry!

"I assume you didn't find the keys," I said.

"Nope," she replied. "Sorry about that. But I'll have another set made in the morning."

"I've got a key," said her father. "You come with me; I'll drive you over to the university and follow you home."

"Gee, Dad," said Mary, "could Mom go instead? I've got a rough day tomorrow and I've got to get some sleep."

"Shakespeare hath murdered sleep!" shouted her father. "Get your coat and c'mon!"

I don't think Mary ever did go to bed that night; by the time they got home she had remembered a term paper due the next day, and she settled herself at the kitchen table to grind it out.

I'm really concerned about the future of America. Do you realize that in another decade or two the entire country could be controlled by a group of individuals who haven't slept since they were seventeen?

7

Anyone for Int. Alg. & Trig.?

"I give up!" sighed our daughter Peggy as she tossed her high school catalogue across the dining-room table. "Tomorrow is the last day for registration, and I still don't have any idea what courses I should take. There are so many to choose from!"

"Take a lot of solid subjects," said her older brother Dan, who was also working on his senior high schedule. "That always impresses the teachers, and it looks good on your college application."

"It won't look good if I flunk them," said Peggy. "And I don't know why I should have to take courses I don't care anything about. I'm not trying to impress anybody, and I'm certainly not going to pretend like I'm the Big Brain."

That last was a direct dig at Danny, who considers himself somewhat of a scholar. The fact that none of his teachers concurs with this consideration does not in any way affect Dan's opinion of himself, though it may have affected his opinion of his teachers.

Danny's teachers are noteworthy in many fields, not the least of which is self-control. Not one of them has yet given in to what must be a compelling urge to kill him. For Dan's opinion of himself is not that far off; he is, or could be, a real scholar. Exceptionally well read, he has total recall and can come up with names, dates, events, theories, and formulae quickly and correctly. But he has an aversion to little things, like attending classes and taking tests. In a high school History Bowl, Dan led his team to first place by snapping off answers Henry Kissinger couldn't come up with. Dan not only knew the answers, but he supplemented them with additional interesting facts, causing members of the history department faculty to congratulate Dan's teacher on such an astounding student.

"That boy is brilliant!" mused an upper-level history teacher. "I wonder whose class he will be taking next year?"

"Probably mine," sighed Dan's teacher, "because if Mr. Brilliant doesn't show up for more classes I'm going to flunk him!"

Peggy does not share Dan's egotism, nor has she decided, as he has, what her chosen field shall be. I do feel sorry for high school students today; when someone asks them what career they are going to choose, their minds must be long since made up, for if they neglect to take a particular high school course, their entire college curriculum may be thrown out of whack. The prerequisites for certain college courses are set up as early as sophomore year in high school. So I could sympathize with Peggy's predicament.

I picked up Peg's catalogue and began to browse through

it. No wonder Peggy had gotten discouraged; consider the first paragraph: "A brief rationale of our variable schedule along with the guidelines for you to follow in determining your course load precede the description of each course. Within this description you will find the prerequisite, the time involved, and the credits allocated."

Show me a fourteen-year-old who can understand that statement and I'll show you a kid who doesn't need to go to high school.

The course descriptions were in keeping with the introduction; they sound like college courses. *Probability and Statistics, Politics and Power, Literary Masterpieces, Literature of Decisions, Advanced Television Production, Sociology, Psychology, Distributive Education, War and Peace.* (That last isn't Tolstoy; it's a course on how to be Secretary of State.)

A "lower level" course is Medical I. As this is offered to first-year students, one might assume that it is a course in first aid. And they do learn about first aid. They also study "nursing procedures, basic life support, medical abbreviations and terminology, hospital and sterile procedure, different diseases (their symptoms, treatment, and care), pediatrics, geriatrics, care of the unconscious patient, care of the tracheotomy patient, care of the cast patient, and the psychological effects of death and dying."

Who needs a doctor? Call in your sophomore!

There is also a course called Medical II for "upper level" students. I can't remember what this course encompasses, but I think it includes interning in a general hospital and specializing in surgery.

The course that intrigued me the most was *Int. Alg. & Trig.* As I had a terrible time with algebra when I was in school, I never even thought about trigonometry, a course limited to mathematics scholars. Thus I assumed that a course in-

tegrating algebra and trigonometry must be for the best and
brightest of mathematics students.

On the contrary, the catalogue claims: *"Int. Alg. & Trig.*
is primarily for individuals who have experienced difficulty in
previous courses." This course is for *slow* kids. Can you imagine what the *smart* kids are expected to take?

The catalogue's Foreign Language sections read like a
United Nations directory. Fourteen-year-olds who have not
yet mastered the English language are offered not just the
simple languages like French and Spanish, but also Latin,
Greek, German, Russian, and Hebrew.

When Dan signed up for Latin, I was pleased and surprised. Good old Latin!

"I thought Dan would take Russian," said my husband
when I told him of Dan's choice of Latin.

"Russian! Why Russian?" I asked. "I could see German,
maybe, as that is considered so scholarly. But Russian?"

"The Germans are no longer imperialists," said my husband, "so why learn the language? But one never knows
about the Russians, and Danny's a guy who covers all the
bases. You must admit, Danny would make a great collabo-
rator!"

As Dan and Peg continued to struggle with their sched-
ules, I could not help but remember how simple school was in
my day. On registration day, we didn't pore over catalogues or
confer with counselors as to whether we should take Metals
or Metaphysics. We just showed up on the first day of school
and were told: "These are your classes. Be there." There were
no electives, no special courses, no block systems, no modular
scheduling. There were six hours in the school day, so we
took six classes, the same subjects every year: English, History, Math, Latin, Language, and Science. Latin, of course,
was required.

English was exactly what it purported to be: the English

language spoken, written, and read. And God help anyone who came out of the eighth grade without being fluent in the first two aspects and at least familiar with the third. All incoming freshmen were given an English test, and if one word was misspelled, or one comma misplaced, we got slapped into Freshman English, where we diagrammed sentences, perfected our punctuation, and memorized rules until we were considered qualified to take the literature courses, all of which were entitled *Prose and Poetry*.

Prose and Poetry I, II, III, and IV (pity the poor girl who got hung up in Freshman English; she missed P. and P. IV and thus never got to read *Moby Dick*) consisted of carefully selected poems, short stories, long essays, and dull novels.

Along with our textbooks, we were given two booklists: one of books we would be required to read throughout the year, and the other of books we were forbidden to read. (The then-famous, but since abolished, INDEX.) Needless to say, we read all the books on the second list and as few as possible on the first list, which made me wonder, in later years, why some clever teacher didn't simply switch lists.

Perhaps one did. A month ago my daughter brought home a book she had been assigned for English class, and I was surprised to see that it was a novel I had sneaked into my college dormitory and read beneath the blankets, blushing furiously throughout and burning on completion lest those hallowed halls be tainted by its very presence. Yesterday I noticed that the book is still sitting on my daughter's desk, so I asked her if she had read it.

"No," she admitted. "It's too long and too dull."

"But how can you write a report on it if you don't read it?" I asked her.

"No problem," she said. "It's going to be on television next week; I'll write the report on the TV version."

"That story is going to be portrayed on television?" I asked incredulously. "Not on prime time, I hope!"

"No," she said, "as a matter of fact, it's going to be animated on Saturday-morning cartoons."

Ah, these modernists! What a clever way of assuring themselves of an audience!

My high school history courses consisted of American, English, Church, and World history, the last so comprehensive we forgot more than we retained. We retained nothing at all of our math courses, because in those days girls weren't expected to comprehend such things as algebra and geometry, though both were required for entrance into college. The girls who were not college-bound were allowed to take Business Arithmetic, a simple course which earned them the contempt of their college-bound classmates as well as, in later years, the first executive positions for women. (They also became the only housewives who could balance their checkbooks.)

The teachers were equally tolerant about our science courses, giving us passing grades if we learned the meaning of H_2O and remembered to blow out our Bunsen burners.

All of us, however, were expected to excel in languages. Though Spanish was offered, we were advised to take French, which the teachers all spoke fluently and which they considered a universal language. So I took four years of French and have yet to meet anyone who speaks it, except my former classmates, who, whenever we meet, always seem to lapse into English.

Despite the simple schedule of my high school days, I always seemed to be loaded down with studies and felt particularly pressured during exam time. When I realize what heavy loads my own children had assumed, I became concerned, and I wasn't surprised when Peggy's counselor called me to check over her schedule.

"Did you approve these courses?" he asked me.

"Yes, I did," I admitted. "Didn't I sign her card?"

"It's a little difficult to read her card," he said apologetically. "She has made so many changes."

"Changes?" I asked, remembering all the solid subjects Peggy had chosen.

"Yes," he said. "Would you like me to read you her revised schedule?"

"Please do," I told him.

"Band, Basketball, Choir, Glee Club, Ceramics, Watercolors, and Photography."

"How odd," I said. "Do you suppose she is considering a career in art or music?"

"She's not considering a career at all," he said. "When I suggested that to her, she said to heck with it; she isn't going to work for a living. She says she's going to get married and have babies and all she really needs out of school are courses which will complement her hobbies!"

"That sounds pretty good to me," I said. "Can't we let her get away with that?"

"Of course not!" he said with some exasperation. "She has to take a literature course, and a language, and some math—"

"She doesn't need a literature course," I told him. "She watches Saturday-morning cartoons. And as for a language, she speaks English fluently, which is more than you can say for most teenagers today."

"But what about math?" he asked weakly.

"Oh don't worry about math," I told him. "So what if she skips a year? She can always catch up by taking *Int. Alg. & Trig.!*"

8

Runaways

"Have any of your children ever run away from home?" a child psychologist asked me recently.

"Of course not!" I replied with what I hoped was a tone of righteous indignation. (I've spent years trying to achieve a tone of righteous indignation. I'm great with the indignation, but for some reason I can't seem to perfect the righteousness.) I should have told him the truth; our kids would never run away for the simple reason that I would never let them take the car.

Actually, one of our kids did run away one time but I don't like to talk about it, not because it was such a frightening experience, but because it was such an embarrassing one. Our little "runaway" was only nine years old, and, to my shame, I didn't even miss him until he called home in tears, asking us to come and get him.

It was my fault, of course. (Isn't it always?) It was one of those hot, humid afternoons so typical in summertime Nebraska, and I had just come home from the hospital with a new baby, our eighth. Our four older boys, ages six, seven, eight, and nine had been playing demolition derby in our driveway with their neighborhood pals, all on bikes, scooters, or roller skates, and all yelling at the top of their lungs. Our three toddlers, ages five, three, and two, were playing noisily in the upstairs playroom, happily destroying each other's toys. I had just put the baby down for her nap, and in my usual postnatal nervousness (which always seemed to last till the next baby was born), I found myself periodically screaming that I would "kill the first kid who wakes up the baby!"

Now I am really quite fair and just with my screaming. I don't yell at my own kids any louder than I yell at the neighbors' kids, the milkman, the meter reader, or anybody else who dares to be noisy at naptime. But evidently our nine-year-old was feeling very sensitive that day, for he took my screaming seriously and, not wanting to be either quiet or killed, he hopped on his bike and took off.

I should have missed him at supper but, I'm ashamed to say, I didn't. It was one of those stand-up and hurry-up suppers, with a few of the neighborhood kids "eating over," as my husband was taking all those "old enough" to the Little League twilight baseball game. After supper, my husband had hustled the older boys off to the ball park, while I stayed home to care for the little ones and to clean up the kitchen. Even after they all came home from the game, I didn't realize that one of the boys was missing.

About nine o'clock, just as it was growing dark, the telephone rang and a trembly little voice said:

"Can I talk to Daddy?"

"Who is this?" I asked.

"It's me, Mama," wept my little guy. "Can Daddy come and get me?"

"But where are you?" I asked in disbelief. "I thought you were in your room!"

"I'm in a drugstore by a vacant lot that's across the street from a church and I wanna come home but I don't know how to get there!"

I felt terrible. I called his father to the phone, and together we finally figured out where our son was. My husband went to pick up our son, gently chastising him on the way home (. . . and not-so-gently chastising me after they got home).

Since that day, I have taken to counting my kids regularly . . . before and after meals and at bedtime, and sometimes after bedtime, as I did one night some years later.

I awoke about 3 A.M. one hot summer night, and realized that I had forgotten to make my usual body count. So I dragged myself from bedroom to bedroom (no easy task when one child sleeps in a basement bedroom, more sleep on the second floor, and still more sleep on the third floor) counting kids. I came suddenly awake when I realized that I came up one short. Our fifteen-year-old was gone!

He'd run away. I just knew it. We'd just watched a TV special on runaway kids and he had remarked that it looked like fun. Fun! How could he do this to me? I quickly and frantically checked every room in the house; he wasn't anyplace. What should I do? Call the police? The Hot Line for Runaways? The Personal Crisis Service? Or should I do something really drastic . . . like wake up my husband?

For the next hour I paced the floor, wringing my hands and making flying novenas to saints Leocadia, Didacus, and Irenaeous (I never call on the well-known saints; they're bound to be busy). Where was my baby? What had I done to drive him away?

At dawn I opened the front door to calm my panic with the cool morning breeze, and as I stepped out onto our screened-in porch I fell over a body. Our son! Was he dead? No, he was snoring.

"Oh, sweetheart, you've come back!" I cried, throwing myself upon his startled hulk. "Thank God! But where have you been? Why did you leave? Are you unhappy here? Do you feel rejected? What can I do to re-establish our relationship? Raise your allowance? Restock the refrigerator? Cancel your dental appointment? Come inside and we'll communicate!"

"Oh, for cryin' out loud, Mom, leggo me, will you?" He woke up grumpily and reluctantly. "I haven't been anyplace. It got so hot on the third floor I came out on the porch to sleep. What makes you think I would run away?"

Of course he wouldn't run away. He couldn't. He didn't even have a driver's license.

As our children grow older, we don't worry about the possible runaways so much as we do about the possible returns. With five of our ten children now out of high school, and four of them no longer living at home (at least that was the count at ten this morning), we are experiencing what a friend of mine once referred to as "the yo-yo bit."

Do you know why they call college-age kids yo-yos? Because they leave home . . . and they come back home . . . and they leave home again . . . and they come back again. . . . Or they enroll in college, then drop out of college, then go back to college, then drop out of college . . . always dropping out two days after their tuition would have been refunded and always going back two weeks after their father finally got them a job by signing an affidavit that his son is definitely not interested in going back to school and will, therefore, be willing to work there forever.

We have had a couple of kids move to Lincoln, Nebraska (to go to the university; not the penitentiary), and a couple of kids stay home and go to the University of Nebraska at Omaha. What seems to confuse the intercampus registrar (as well as me) is that it's never the same two kids in the same college at the same time.

When our eldest son, Lee, graduated from high school, he didn't want to quit his part-time job, so he stayed home and enrolled at the University of Nebraska at Omaha.

A year later, his brother John graduated from high school and chose to go to the University of Nebraska at Lincoln because, of course, he would not consider going to the same college as his brother.

When our third son, Mike, graduated from high school he won a scholarship to UNL and he enrolled there, whereupon John immediately dropped out and got a job.

The following semester, Lee took off to work for a semester, so John came home and went to UNO, but when Lee went back to UNO, John went back to Lincoln.

By this time their sister Mary had graduated from high school and she, too, wanted to go to Lincoln but she had won a scholarship to UNO, so we made her stay home and go to school here. The following semester, Mike's UNL scholarship ran out, so he transferred to UNO so he could live at home until he could save enough money to go back to Lincoln.

At least, I think that's where he is, and I'm almost sure Mary's the one at UNO. If the registrar, with all his files and all that clerical help can't keep track of my kids, I don't know how he expects me to keep track of them. And I certainly can't keep track of their overdue library books that are constantly holding up the registration of one or the other of them but nobody knows which one because my kids learned long ago to always check out their books on the other kid's card.

Another of our sons, Jim, chose not to go to college. The fourth of our "terrible toddlers," Jim spent most of his childhood years being buffeted, bribed, threatened, and beat up by his three awful older brothers, whom he nevertheless adored and whom he followed everywhere, always and faithfully doing their bidding. The only place he chose not to follow them was into college; he opted instead for military service. Jim enlisted in the United States Marine Corps, where he learned judo, karate, hand-to-hand combat, and guerrilla tactics, not in anticipation of war but in anticipation of his visits home. To his chagrin, his older brothers have now lost interest in antagonizing him. (I wonder why.)

Even with Jim in the Marines, and our older son now married, our adult children seem to "yo" home at regular intervals, or at least frequently enough to confuse the neighbors.

As I was working in the back yard yesterday afternoon, my neighbor Mary Jo waved and called:

"I see Mike's home for a visit!"

"Not Mike," I replied. "John's home for a few days."

"Oh," she said, strolling over into my yard, "I didn't realize that John wears glasses."

"John isn't the one you saw with the glasses," I explained. "That's Jim; he's home on leave."

"He sure has a pretty wife," she said.

"Jim doesn't have a wife," I told her. "You must mean his sister-in-law."

"John's wife?" she asked. "I didn't know John was married."

"John *isn't* married," I told her, suddenly realizing that I hadn't seen John yet this morning; could he have eloped last night? "The girl you saw is Lee's wife, Karen; they were here for Easter."

"Well, it must be nice to have them all home. . . ."

"But they're not all home," I interrupted her. "Mike's away at college, and . . ."

"Then who's that coming around the corner of your house?" asked Mary Jo, obviously puzzled.

"Hi, Ma!" yelled Mike cheerfully, as he swung his duffel

bag onto the porch. "I got a couple of days off, so I thought I would come home and chow down!"

"That's wonderful," I said, swallowing a sigh. "I'll take another steak out of the freezer."

I wish I had spent more time listening to that child psychologist. Maybe I would have learned something about runaways.

Like how to grow one.

9

This Is a Vacation?

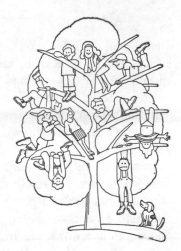

"I am so mad!" my neighbor Nancy complained the other day as we shared a pitcher of lemonade on my back-yard patio.

"Why? What's the matter?" I asked.

"This is the first summer that I am not working, and we had planned an automobile trip with our kids. But now my husband tells me that with the price of gasoline so high, we can't go. Which means that I am going to be cooped up at home through this entire summer with my kids! Can you imagine anything worse?"

"As a matter of fact, I can," I told her.

"What?" she asked.

"Taking an automobile trip with your kids," I said. "Your trouble, Nancy, is your lack of experience. You've never driven your kids farther than the playground. You haven't *lived* until you have spent ten days in transit with kids who outnumber the car windows."

As a mother of ten children, I feel qualified, maybe even obligated, to warn young parents of the hazards of family life, and I can't think of a hazard more horrible than "the family vacation."

One of the main problems involved in traveling with children is their age. When children are young, they are enthusiastic and excited about going on a trip, but it is unlikely that they will appreciate the trip. When they finally grow old enough to appreciate the trip, they won't want to go.

In spite of it all, we parents keep trying to entertain and educate our children by cooping them up in a car and taking them to the mountains (which we will worry about them falling off of), the ocean (which we will worry about them falling into), or "the big city" where we take them to museums, galleries, theaters, and restaurants, which are exactly like those in our own hometown but which we have never bothered to take them to.

As my fear of height is exceeded only by my terror of water, we have never taken our children to either the mountains or the seashore, but we have, on a couple of occasions, made the mistake of taking them to "the big city" to see the sights.

With ten children, it is not only impractical but impossible to take a vacation *en famille,* so we split our offspring into two groups, taking the little children one summer and the teenagers the next.

I don't know which was worse.

For the little children, we had planned a trip to Kansas City, an ideal town for a family vacation, for there is Worlds of Fun for the kids, the Royals baseball games for Dad, and the many museums for Mom. It is particularly ideal for us, as we live in Omaha . . . close enough that we could endure the three-hour ride with our kids and far enough for the kids to consider it a "real trip."

We knew it could be expensive, so we planned our budget carefully. We chose a "Discount Day" at Worlds of Fun, Family Night at the ball park, and we made reservations in one of those "affordable" motels.

My first hint that the trip would be paved with stumbling blocks occurred when we prepared to pack our bags, and I realized that my kids had evidently spent the first six weeks of the summer dressed in rags. (Why is it that we never look at our children until we think someone else is going to look at them?) So our first "unexpected expense" was new clothes for all. I took the kids to the shopping center and bought shorts and T-shirts, swimsuits and sneakers, and an unfamiliar garment which, I explained to them, bore the unusual name of "pajamas" and are often worn at night by civilized peoples who consider it uncouth to sleep in their underwear.

At last the purchases were made, the packing completed, and we were off.

Boy, were we off.

I had been warned of the trauma of traveling with children, and I was prepared for a certain amount of scuffling and shoving, car sickness and boredom. What I was not prepared for was twenty-three stops to check out the roadside restrooms and, on one occasion, a dense clump of bushes for a little kid who couldn't wait.

Why is it that a little boy, who went through his entire kindergarten career without finding the boys' lavatory, cannot travel for ten miles without heeding nature's call?

Due to these unexpected stops, we made the three-hour journey in slightly under five hours. On arriving at our motel, we soon realized why it had been advertised as "affordable." There was no swimming pool, no coffee shop, and no television. Such austerity did not affect its popularity, however. On checking in, we were told that the party using our reserved three-room suite had decided to stay another week, and we would have to settle for two tiny rooms and some supplemental cots.

I rebelled. It's all I can do to stay sane in our ten-room home where I can, when necessary, separate squabbling siblings or even take myself into hiding in our third-floor master bedroom. I was not about to spend three days sharing two tiny rooms with six kids and their crazy father. True, he wasn't crazy yet, but he would have been by midnight.

The only other accommodations available proved to be in Kansas City's swankiest hotel, where we could house our family comfortably for only a little less money than it would have cost us to buy a home in Mission Hills. I convinced my husband that it would be worth it, offering him my old-time favorite argument: "You'd rather pay for my psychiatric treatments?"

The hotel is truly luxurious, and I could hardly bring myself to leave it the next morning to accompany the family to Worlds of Fun. That famous amusement park is as glorious as the brochures promise, but I think you should know that, aside from the super rides, exotic shops, and grand entertainers, there is a very popular game often played in the park. This game is called Looking for Your Kids.

While our sons dashed madly from ride to ride, seeking greater and greater thrills, and our daughters strolled from shop to shop, seeking more places to spend our money, my husband and I frantically tried to keep track of them. Nobody wanted to go in the same direction at the same time, and our cries of "Meet us at the snack bar in an hour!" had little effect, as there are so many snack bars . . . and nobody had a watch but Mom and Dad.

We somehow managed to make it through the day, but disaster hovered, shortly before departure time, when we had all assembled and suddenly realized that nobody had seen our youngest child for the past two hours. He was missing, and he was alone.

How could that happen? The brother who was assigned to watch him had foisted that responsibility off on to his sister, who had asked another sister to watch him "for just a second." And she had. Literally. She watched him for "just a second." (I told her not to cry; her little brother has been known to disappear in half that time.)

Rather than run the risk of getting separated again by fanning out to search, we decided the best thing to do was go to the Security Office for help. There we found our little son, adamantly proclaiming to the officer:

"For the last time, Mister; I am *not* lost. I know exactly where I am. I just don't know where my family is; *they* are the ones who are lost!"

The next day we took a tour of Kansas City to see the lovely homes, the well-planned parkways, the fabulous Country Club Plaza, the famous fountains, and Swope Park, and that evening we went to the long-anticipated Royals baseball game in the magnificent Truman Sports Complex. It was a perfect night for a game: clear and cool, and we had excellent seats. All the "star" players were scheduled to participate in this exciting game with New York.

Unfortunately, we didn't get to see the game. We had to leave in the second inning to keep from being annihilated by the crowd. No, there was no pushing and shoving; the stadium is roomy and comfortable. It's just that Royals fans do not take too well to six kids screaming: "Yeah, Yankees! Cream Kansas City!"

The last day of our trip we drove out to Independence to visit the Truman Library, which houses the presidential papers, pictures, and artifacts of a most fascinating, if controversial, President. However, we didn't get to see any of the papers, pictures, or artifacts, because we got thrown out of the place when our ten-year-old broke into the presidential limousine and pretended to drive it, while his eleven-year-old brother "rode" the running board shouting: "Hail to the Chief!"

While I could understand the reactions of the staid security guards, I could not help but think that had old Harry been there himself, he would have enjoyed the whole show and probably would never have let them assess us for the damage to the door handle. After all, it was an old car!

So the vacation was a fiasco, but we assumed that this was due to the fact that the kids were too young for such a venture. If you don't think we were mistaken, try a trip with your teenagers.

10

On the Road Again . . .

There is one important factor which parents should take into consideration before venturing on a vacation with teenagers and that is: they really do not want to go. While you and I may consider gazing down the Grand Canyon an exciting experience, teenagers consider that particular Wonder of the World just another gap in the ground, and they would much prefer to spend their time doing something worthwhile, like sleeping, or listening to punk-rock records, or watching reruns of "Saturday Night Live."

I knew that our teenagers would be reluctant to take a vacation with their father and me, but I felt that once we were on the way they would cooperate and participate and maybe even enjoy themselves. I called them together and told them the news.

"I've got a surprise for you," I said. "Your father and I are going to take you to Chicago!"

"Why?" asked one son.

"What do you mean 'Why?'" I laughed. "To see the sights, of course! We'll show you the Loop, and we'll go through the Museum of Science and Industry. We'll drive up Sheridan Road and see the many mansions and universities. We'll even take a boat ride on Lake Michigan! It'll be great fun!

"Don't you want to go?" I asked, which was a dumb thing to do, but I'm not so dumb that I waited for a reply. "Of course you are going. We'll have a terrific time! Now I want you to check over your clothes and see what you will need new before we pack our bags." I wasn't about to make the same mistake I had made with their younger siblings. This time, we would be prepared.

The boys dutifully inventoried their belongings, then borrowed my credit cards and went to the shopping center to supplement their wardrobes.

"Did you remember to buy pajamas?" I asked them when they returned, laden with packages.

"Pajamas?" they asked. "Do you mean we are going all the way to Chicago just to go to bed? We can sleep at home! Who's gonna need pajamas?"

"Well, what did you buy?" I asked, and they reluctantly revealed their purchases: two six-packs of pop, a triple bag of potato chips, twelve candy bars, a carton of cigarettes, four pounds of lunch meat, and three loaves of sandwich bread, a jar of dill pickles, four rock albums, and four magazines, the covers of which should have melted the candy, curdled the pickles, and blown up the pop.

I confiscated the magazines (which I burned before my husband decided to "censor" them), told the boys I was glad they had bought the food because I knew they would get

hungry while traveling, and if there is anything more discon-
certing than stopping every few miles for a little kid to use a
restroom, it is stopping every few miles so a big kid can eat.

I even supplemented their supply with a chocolate cake,
some cookies, and a thermos of coffee, figuring that between
their purchases and my baked goods they would have enough
food to last them halfway across the state of Iowa.

It lasted them halfway across the city of Omaha. Consequently, we had to stop in Council Bluffs for brunch, in
Avoca for a snack break, in Des Moines for lunch, in Iowa
City for a milkshake, and in Davenport for a sandwich to sustain them till suppertime.

We checked into a lovely motel in Lincolnwood, and before we had the car unpacked, the kids had found the pop
machine, the ice machine, the candy machine, and the telephone, which they used to order "just a couple of things"
from room service.

I finally sent them to their own rooms, with the admonish-
ment to "dress for dinner," as we had made reservations at a
very swanky supper club. To my delight, they met us in the
lobby an hour later, each dressed in neat slacks, sport coat,
and tie. They looked so handsome, I could hardly wait to
show them off!

We drove to the club, parked the car, and entered the ele-
gant foyer, where a distinguished maître d' approached to ask
for our reservations.

"I'm so sorry," he said as he surveyed our handsome sons,
"but I cannot seat you."

"Why not?" asked my husband. "We have reservations
and, anyway, the dining room is practically empty. You can't
tell me all those tables were reserved ahead of ours!"

"It's not a question of reservations, monsieur," said the
maître d'. "It's our dress code. The young gentlemen do not
meet our dress code."

"Of course they do!" said my husband firmly. "They're wearing coats, and ties—"

"I know, monsieur," interrupted the maître d' quietly, "but they are not wearing socks. I'm sorry, but we do insist on socks. Perhaps you will find the cafeteria across the street to your liking."

Swell. I travel five hundred miles and get all dolled up in a long gown, just so I can carry my own tray.

It didn't bother the boys, however. They were delighted to eat in the cafeteria, for they knew that that swank supper club wouldn't have given them a choice of twelve entrees, and let them choose all twelve.

The next day we took a boat ride on Lake Michigan, where I got soaked and the boys got hungry, an elevator ride to the top of the John Hancock building, where I got dizzy and the boys got candy bars, and a tour of an art gallery, which proved to be a disaster. The art was superb, but the vending machines were broken.

And where was their father during all this? Trying to find a parking place, of course. Haven't you ever been to Chicago?

I was sure that the next day would be better, as we were going to visit the Museum of Science and Industry, a magnificent place where even the dumbest kid can become enthralled (and the most impatient father can find a place to park).

We had, in fact, allotted several days to the museum, for as anyone knows, it is impossible to view all the attractions in one afternoon. I knew the boys would want to see the section on the space age and the one on the Industrial Revolution. They would want to investigate all the latest electronic gadgets, and walk through the submarine, and venture down the 1910 city street. They would love it!

They hated it. The snack bar was closed.

That was the last time we attempted a family vacation, and

while many parents claim they dread the summer because they will be cooped up with their kids, I do not. For my husband and I have found the perfect solution to the problem of spending twenty-four hours a day, seven days a week, with one's children. The solution was so obvious, I don't know why we didn't see it long ago. It's so natural. Our solution?

During the summer months, from Memorial Day to Labor Day, we sleep all night, and the kids sleep all day.

11

Call In a Mechanic!

Last year my husband (the last of the Great Romantics) gave me a toaster for Christmas. I shouldn't disparage this practical gift, for I had put a toaster at the top of my Most Wanted List, as might any mother who has spent years trying to make toast for twelve in a two-slice appliance.

But while I had hoped to get a toaster for Christmas, I had not expected the toaster I got. It was a four-slice variety, all right, but in place of the simple "push down" bar, there was a panel of controls complicated enough to run the entire Strategic Air Command.

On the lower-left corner was a color-choice knob, offering light, medium, dusk, or dark, and opposite that was a knob to choose the texture of the toast: firm, soft, or someplace-in-between. A heat-control thermostat could be adjusted for frozen bread, fresh bread, stale bread, pastry, and even buns, while yet another knob set the toaster on "keep warm" (for the benefit of the kid who is still upstairs looking for his socks). There was a clip to open the panel so one could clean the crumb tray (just in case the toaster ever got into the hands of a housewife who cleans her crumb trays), while two more knobs seemed to be meaningless; perhaps they were just for decoration.

"This is a terrific toaster," I told my husband sincerely, "but it's so complicated, I'll never get the hang of it."

"That's what the directions are for," he said. "Aren't there directions with it?"

"Sixteen pages of them," I said, as I riffled through the booklet, "four pages in Japanese, four in German, four in some language that looks like Swedish, and four pages of diagrams which do not bear the faintest resemblance to this appliance. I think the Japanese have finally wreaked their revenge for World War II."

"You shouldn't need directions," said my husband. "It's just a toaster; anybody should be able to figure out how it works."

By eight the next morning I was ready to send out for Anybody. I had spent forty-five minutes decoding the color control, interpreting the texture regulator, solving the secret of the thermostat, checking out the crumb tray, and puzzling over the two mystery switches, which I finally realized were for "on" and "off." But I had set and reset all the switches in varying shades, textures, and temperatures to no avail. The toaster would not work.

When my husband came down to breakfast, I said: "You'll have to return this toaster; it's defective. I think there is something the matter with the heating element. The bread keeps popping up bread."

My husband turned the toaster over and around and up-side down, checking knobs, switches, and controls, and then said: "You're right; it's the heating element. It won't heat unless you plug it in."

Well how was I to remember that, when the plug and cord were neatly tucked out of sight and mind in that hidden compartment?

I admit that I am not electronically oriented, but maybe that is because I was raised in an era when electronics had not yet entered the dictionary, let alone the common kitchen. My mother's tutoring in the art of homemaking did not prepare me for a transistorized world controlled almost entirely by push-button panels created by an Oriental mind.

My mother had it easy. For example, when she wanted to beat an egg, all she had to do was turn the handle of her "portable" egg beater. (She didn't know it was "portable," of course; she just knew it didn't plug in. "Portable," like "electronics," was a future word.) Today, when I want to beat an egg, I have to dig through the cabinets and pull out a cumbersome blender (which is usually coated with chocolate from the last time the kids made shakes), then try to figure out how to "beat" when the buttons say "Stir," "Blend," "Mix," "Whip," "Chop," "Mince," "Grate," "Grind," "Shred," "Cream," "Frappé," and "Liquefy," but not, of course, "Beat."

My automatic washing machine was advertised as a "Miracle Machine," the miracle being, I could only conclude after using it, that it can soak, wash twice, and rinse thrice without getting the clothes clean. (Where, oh, where is Durwood Kirby?) I fear it is due to the fact that I can't figure out the panel on the machine. There are seventeen push buttons (none of which say "wash" or even "on") and I can't decipher the sixty-page book of directions because it covers thirteen

models made by this manufacturer but not, methinks, my
model.

If anything goes wrong with my washing machine
(frankly, I'm still waiting for something to go right), I must
call a repairman, for only someone with a Ph.D. in engineering could possibly understand so complicated a machine.

You can be sure my mother never had such frustrations
with *her* washing machine, though it didn't have an "on" but-
ton either. It didn't have any buttons, switches, or knobs. All
it had was a hose which attached to the faucet over the basement sink. If her machine refused to fill with water, it was
simply because she had forgotten to turn on the faucet. If her
machine flooded, she just pulled the plug at the bottom of the
machine.

And if the machine refused to drain, all she had to do was
plunge her arm into the water and fish around with her
fingers until she found the elusive sock that was blocking the
drain. (Her old washing machine was somewhat of a social
climber; it tried to be a "sock-eater" like its sophisticated
sisters of today.)

The clothes washed in Mother's machine always got clean,
if only out of fear. They knew that if they didn't, she'd beat
them to death on the washboard. I tried to intimidate my
clothes by placing a washboard in plain sight in my laundry
room, but it didn't do any good. My clothes know very well I
am not about to grate my knuckles on that monstrosity.

It isn't just the toaster and the washing machine that defeat
me; it's also the iron (Mother's could be adjusted to "on" and
"off"; mine has a list of settings only a scientist could interpret), the refrigerator (with its ice maker, ice crusher, self-
defrost, humidistat, meat keeper, vegetable keeper, cola
keeper . . . none of which work properly because, the repairman keeps telling me, I use them incorrectly) and the range,
where I can only use one burner because all the others are au-

tomatic, thermostatic, or just coated with guck, which I can't clean because I can't figure out how to take the darn thing apart.

I can't take the burners apart because my ignorance of things mechanical equals my ignorance of things electronic. A tool in my hand is as out of place as a missal in Madalyn Murray O'Hair's. I don't know a vice-grip from a monkey wrench, and I prefer to think of a screwdriver as a tasty orange drink.

I grew up in an era when tools were masculine. Except for a garden trowel or pruning shears, a lady never handled tools. My mother never in her life changed a tire, or repaired an electric outlet, or took apart the trap under the kitchen sink. Her talent lay in the culinary, rather than the industrial, and while she could quote verbatim from the most comprehensive cookbook, she could never interpret the simplest mechanic's manual.

So perhaps it is not surprising that I grew up thinking that "my place" was in the kitchen and not the basement workshop. But if I had it to do over, I would forgo home economics for shop class, for while modern technology has progressed considerably in the fields of ready-to-eat foods and ready-to-wear clothes, it has regressed miserably in the area of ready-to-use toys.

Just think about it. How long has it been since you purchased a toy that did not have to be put together? (My sister claims that the only thing that comes preassembled these days is a baby.)

Take bicycles, for example. In my day, when a child reached the age where he could ride a bicycle, his dad took him to the bike shop, where he picked out a bike and rode it home.

Not anymore. Today, when a child is old enough to ride a bicycle, you take him to the bike shop where you choose the make, model, and color you can afford (it's never the one the kid wants), wait six weeks for the order to be delivered, then go back to the bike shop to pick up a tightly sealed carton containing 1,746 parts. You then lug the carton home and spend the next three days assembling the bicycle.

For years, the assembling of the Bloomingdale bicycles was the task of my talented-with-tools husband, but the last time we bought a bicycle, he was out of town, and I got stuck with the job.

We had ordered a new bike for Patrick for his birthday, and when the bike shop called to say our order was in, Patrick insisted that we not wait for his father to come home to assemble the bike.

"Let's go get the bike and bring it home," said Pat. "I'll help you put it together."

Realizing that my eleven-year-old Pat was about as handy with tools as his mother, I called the bike shop and asked them if they would do me a favor and assemble the bike for me.

"Sure," the clerk said cheerfully. "Be happy to. It'll cost you twenty-five dollars and I can have it ready for you a week from Thursday."

I was not about to pay twenty-five dollars to assemble that bicycle; I had already paid more for that bike than my Grandpa Cooney paid for his Pontiac, also, I knew Pat could not wait another week.

So Patrick and I drove to the bike shop, lugged the huge carton home, and dumped it in the driveway, where I planned to put it together.

"We have to get this carton open, Pat," I said. "Run inside and bring me something to cut it open with."

Pat quickly went into the house and returned with a pair of my best manicure scissors.

"No, no, Patrick, this won't do," I said. "I need something stronger."

Patrick found a screwdriver and kitchen shears, and to-gether we managed to pry the carton open and spill the contents onto the ground, only to discover that there were no directions.

I called the bike shop and complained.

"You don't need directions," insisted the clerk. "All you have to do is put the frame together, bolt on the handlebars and seat, slip on the pedals, and there you go. It's so simple a child could do it."

A child could do it. I hate it when they tell me that. A child can also open the spout on cake-mix boxes and flip the safety caps off medicine bottles, neither of which I can do.

But at Patrick's insistence, I went to work on the bike. (Now you may well wonder where Patrick's teenage brothers were when all this was going on. Why weren't they around to help? If I knew the manner and means by which teenage boys manage to disappear when there is work to be done, I wouldn't be writing this silly book. I'd be writing a best-seller.)

I finally got the frame together only to discover that the handlebars veered south by southwest. I took them off and put them back on again. North by northeast. Try again. We finally got the handlebars squared away, when the back wheel fell off. No fair! That was supposed to be factory-installed! We got the wheel back on, slipped on the pedals, bolted on the seat, and then faced the hardest task of all: the handlebar grips.

I have endured ten tenures of tricycles, and I am well aware of the handlebar-grip phenomena. The diameter of the handlebars is always about two millimeters larger than the diameter of the grips. You can push, pull, tug, and shove, but the grips will not fit onto the bars.

As I was tugging away at this impossible task, my sixteen-year-old daughter, Peggy, came walking up the driveway.

"Whatcha doin', Mom?" she asked cheerfully.

"What does it look like I'm doing?" I asked sarcastically, as I switched grips in the futile hope that the left might be larger than the right.

"If you're trying to get those handlebar grips on," she said, "you're going about it the wrong way."

"And I suppose you know the right way?" I asked.

"Sure," she said confidently. "Just soak the grips in hot water till they soften up a little, then lightly grease the handlebars and the grips should slip right on."

"Where did you learn that?" I asked in genuine awe.

"In Home Economics Class," she said.

"In Home Ec?" I asked. "I thought all they taught there was cooking and sewing."

"That's just the first semester," she said. "During the second semester we study Home Repairs, Auto Mechanics, and the Assembling of Home Appliances. Things have changed since your day, Mom."

I'll say. In my day, bike handlebars grew their own grips.

I finally got the bike together, and when my husband saw it, he was so proud of me he threatened to give me a fully equipped workshop for Christmas.

"If you give me a workshop, I'll give you a divorce," I said. "For Christmas this year, I want a gift that is pretty, and expensive, and totally feminine. Furthermore, I don't want anything useful!"

He followed my instructions to the letter. He gave me a beautiful and expensive purse, which is totally useless because I can't figure out the tricky clasp, or find the secret compartment, or unsnap the stubborn key chain, or disentangle the photo-ident-credit-card case, or fit my checkbook into the designated pocket.

Next year I am going to ask him for a diamond ring, and I won't even care if it comes unassembled.

12

The Victory Garden Surrenders

I may very well be exiled from the state of Nebraska for making this statement, but my conscience, as well as my aching back, compel me to do so.

I am not a farmer.

Despite the fact that I have lived for the past quarter century in this most fertile and fruitful agricultural state, enjoying their hospitality and basking in their agrarian pride, I do not share their love of the soil. I do not like to dig in the dirt; I do not find fulfillment in sowing seeds and reaping harvests. I do not want to be a farmer, even an amateur farmer.

I have nothing against farmers, you understand. As a matter of fact, I love them dearly, for they make it possible for me to indulge in my favorite pastime: eating. I even envy farmers their talents; I just don't share those talents. If I want to enjoy a succulent tomato, a crisp lettuce salad, or a fresh ear of hot, buttered corn, I shall go to the grocer and buy them . . . or, better yet, to the restaurant and order them. What I won't do, because I can't do, is grow them.

I am not ashamed of the fact that I do not have a green thumb; I happily admit that I do not even want a green thumb. What I do not want even more than a green thumb is a back-yard garden.

Why, then, have I spent the past three months ankle deep in fertilized mud, being eaten by insects, suffocated by bug spray, scratched by cucumber vines, intimidated by corn-stalks, and infuriated by rabbits who raced me to the lettuce and won?

Because I am married to a native Nebraskan, that's why.

When I left my home state of Missouri to come to college in Nebraska, I was led to believe that not all Nebraskans are farmers. Some are ranchers, some are professional people, some run small-town businesses. Rumor had it that there were even some folk, born and bred in the city of Omaha, who had never set foot in a cornfield, or placed their hand upon a plow, or awakened to a rooster's crow, or listened to a child cry: "Detassle? In this heat? You've got to be kidding!"

What I didn't learn, until too late, was that even the most sophisticated city-bred Nebraskan thinks of himself as a thwarted farmer and thus feels compelled, upon seeing a patch of unplanted ground, to sow something . . . anything . . . but preferably something edible.

During my college days, I dated indiscriminately: farm boys, ranchers, even football players, but when the time came to marry and settle down, I, aware of my allergy to agriculture, chose my spouse with great care. I opted for an academician, an attorney who was happy only in the courtroom or the classroom. Surely my law-professor husband would be too preoccupied with legal tomes to take an interest in tomatoes.

And, in fact, for the next two decades my husband showed no interest in growing anything other than children, a hobby we shared with equal enthusiasm.

So you can imagine my surprise when, after twenty-some gardenless summers, he came home from the office one afternoon toting, along with his briefcase, a spade, a hoe, and a thirty-five-dollar book entitled *How to Grow Your Own Supper.*

"I have always wanted to have a back-yard garden!" said he, as he pulled a dozen packages of seeds from his briefcase, and for some strange reason, at the sight of the seeds, my fingers began to stiffen, my head to throb, my back to ache. *Déjà vu!*

Suddenly I was back in the summer of 1942. The Second World War was upon us, and for reasons which escape me now and probably escaped me even then, every American was encouraged to have a Victory Garden. My mother, who was always three thoughts ahead of everybody else in town, determined that *our* Victory Garden would not be a personal patch-of-ground-in-our-back-yard type of thing, but rather a four-acre plot where we would grow vegetables to supplement the school-lunch program. No more would we kiddies be forced to brown-bag it with "those terribly monotonous, dreary" (absolutely delicious!) peanut butter and jelly sandwiches and "stale, crumbly" (oh-so-yummy!) potato chips. From henceforth, the school children would have a *nourishing* (the very word should have warned us) lunch of such delectable dishes as hot, buttered green beans, spinach casserole, and turnips au gratin. (Turnips, au yuck!)

The lunch would be offered at an incredibly low price because Mother had kept the overhead down by using incredibly low labor. No pay is about as low pay as you can get, and we, her dutiful if reluctant children, were the overworked and nonpaid laborers.

Throughout those wartime summers, my brother and sisters and I plowed and planted, watered and weeded, picked and pulled, and finally reaped the harvest, which we then hauled over to the school kitchen where we spent our evenings husking the corn, snapping the beans, hulling the peas, and hiding the turnips. (It was bad enough we had to grow the things; we weren't about to eat them, too.)

My back still aches when I remember all that plowing and planting; my fingers stiffen as I recall the husking and the hulling; and my head throbs when I think of what the other kids called us everytime they had to eat that spinach casserole.

When I grew up, I learned to eat and even enjoy the green beans and the spinach (not the turnips; I'm not that far gone), but I am convinced that this is due not to a change in my own tastes, but rather a change in the vegetables themselves. Those prewashed, prepackaged, and sometimes even precooked vegetables that come from the supermarket are much more tempting than the muddy, grubby things dug up out of one's own back yard.

My husband shook me from my reverie with an enthusiastic:

"This is going to be great fun, as well as a real budget saver. We'll make it a family project. I just love to watch things grow!"

And that's what he did. He watched.

While Danny plowed and Timmy planted and Peggy watered and Annie weeded and Patrick chased the rabbits out of the cabbage patch, their father sat proudly on the patio and supervised. Since the patio is on the opposite side of the house from the garden, the supervision tended to be sparse, which probably explains why Danny plowed only half the garden and Timmy planted the other half; why Peggy watered the weeds and Annie pulled the beans (they do look a little like weeds; taste like them, too, says Annie) and Patrick chased the rabbits into the basement where he kept them in hiding until they had increased and multiplied and filled the furnace room.

In spite of it all, we did grow vegetables . . . sort of. It might have helped had anybody taken the time and trouble to read the thirty-five-dollar book on *How to Grow Your Own Supper*, which I am sure would have told us that one cannot grow corn on the shady side of the house, and that tomatoes should be staked lest they get stepped on and sprayed lest they be eaten up by insects, or that cucumbers should be planted sparingly. To this day Timmy, ever loyal to his father, will not "remember" how many cucumber seeds his father told him to sow. Suffice it to say that throughout that entire summer neither we nor the neighbors for three houses north of us had to mow our back yards, for the grass was choked to death by a rapid and continuous growth of cucumber vines.

Unfortunately, our tomatoes did not fare so well, as they were overshadowed by the cornstalks which did, indeed, "grow as high as an elephant's eye," but which did not, however, guarantee an abundance of corn. We had a bushel of ears but nary an ear was over three inches long. We never did discover the reason for this and I am not about to research the subject, lest my beloved back-yard farmer insist we try again next year.

It was with great relief that I welcomed the first frost, and at the first opportunity I cleared the garden of cornstalks and cucumber vines and turned the soil so that, come spring, the crabgrass could once again take over our yard.

And with that statement I have most certainly doomed myself to exile, for if there is anything Nebraskans herald more than their beloved gardens, it is their lovely lawns, carpeted with expensive, carefully cultivated bluegrass.

How can they expect me to grow bluegrass, when I can't even remember to call my yard a "lawn"?

13

A Few of Their Favorite Things

I admit that I am probably the only mother in America who doesn't own a cookbook. I have owned a few, over the years . . . one given to me as a shower gift by my friend Rita, with whom I had shared an apartment (and meals); another given to me, anonymously, as a wedding present (I have always suspected my mother-in-law); another given to me five years later by an embarrassed mother (mine); and still another cookbook came my way one Christmas, a gift from a hungry husband (alas, also mine). Last year, to commemorate my twenty-fifth wedding anniversary, my kids gave me *The Better Homes and Gardens Beginner's Cookbook*. I was not amused.

I have managed to dispose of each and every cookbook by "losing" them, donating them to book fairs, or giving them to my daughter-in-law, who is too polite to tell me she doesn't want them.

The truth is, cookbooks depress me. No matter how few the ingredients, or how simple the steps, the recipes simply don't work for me. I always expect the finished product to look like the picture in the cookbook, and of course it never does.

I even tried the pictureless cookbooks, those "home recipe" books compiled by churches, hospital guilds, et cetera, and sold to raise funds for their organizations. They always claim these books contain "easy, simple recipes" created by women who hate to cook as much as I do. If these are such simple recipes, how come you usually need thirty-two ingredients to make spaghetti? I still buy those cookbooks, because they are fund-raisers for good causes, but I always give them away as quickly as possible, lest my family find them and suggest I use them.

I avoid all cookbooks, whether they be gourmet, economy meals, best-sellers, freebies, or tear-out sections from magazines or newspapers. But recently a cookbook came across my kitchen and warmed my heart, if not my oven. Entitled *A Few of Our Favorite Things*, it was composed as a Mother's Day gift by a first-grade class at St. Joseph's Co-Cathedral School, in St. Joseph, Missouri, and I supplement it here with some choice recipes from the primary students at St. Joan of Arc School, in Omaha, Nebraska. While the recipes are a delight, I must tell you that I recommend them for your reading enjoyment only . . . cook and eat at your own risk!

To preserve the "flavor," the recipes are printed exactly as they were written by the children.

TACOS
Firs you cook the Tacos shell for a hour then you take the Tacos shell out of the oven. If you have some taomatoes, then

you put them in a bowl. Then you take out some hanbuger if you have some hanbuger. Then you put it in a pan. Then you take salad if you have some salad. Then you take some cheez if you have some. Then you domp it all in the shell.

TOSSED SALAD

Tear stuff up and put in dish. Put salad dressing on it.

CHICKEN

Get chicken from store and unwrap it. Put some powder on it. Put it in a pan. Turn oven to 15 degrees and cook until bell rings.

MASKETTI AND MEAT BALLS

Go to store and buy some meat and make it into balls about the size of your mouth. Put balls in frying pan on stove—wait until meat is done. Take off stove and put in big bowl. Buy strips of long hard masketti and put in pot of water. Turn oven on and wait till it is done. Take off stove and put in bowl with meat balls. Mix together.

STEAK

½ onion cut into small pieses and a steak. If you want to BAR B Q it heres what you do. First ask a grown up to get charkol and a BAR B Q and then sprinkel the onoin pieses on top and get the BAR B Q and put the steak on the BAR B Q and thats all.

BAULD EGGS

Get how many eaggs you whant then put them in a pot then boyl them ontell thay bubul than put an X on them then put them in a furgator.

SWETROLLS

Get a taub of Pilsberry swet rools makeings. Bake it. Het it for 800 hours then take it out. Eat.

POP

You put pop in a glass and you can put apples or graps in it and its good.

CAKE

Take two cups water. Stir into the black stuff that makes it good. Put in pan. Put in oven. Turn oven to boil.

MAKRONY

You cook it. Poot it in a dish. Then you let the water out. Then you cook it a leetle moor then you poot it in a plate.

CHOCOLATE COOKIES WITH
PEANUTS AND GRAY STUFF

2½ yards peanut butter; 1,000 or more peanuts; 30 chocolate rectangles. Mix all together. Put in pans. Cook 1,000 seconds at 30 degrees.

CHOCOLATE CHIP COOKIES

1 cup cinnamon sugar; 1 cup milk; 1 bag chocolate chips. Stir it up. Take a spoon. Row dough into balls. Put in pan. Then put in oven at 1 degree. Turn light on in oven. Open and close door until they're done.

STRABERRY CAKE

You get a bakeing pan. Put creme in the pan. Get the doe and rowl it. Make shere that you put the straberrys in the creme. Now its time for the fynle part. Put the shuger in. Then you put the doe in the shuger then you put the cake in the pan then you put the pan in to bake for 20 mints. Then the cake is done.

PIZZA
Put 2 cupos of flowers and 1 cupo of shuger and a stick of butter and mix it with a egg beter. Cook hamger and tomado joos and when its dun put it on the crust. Then put meet on and lots of Greenoluvs and Aunt Chevys.

GERMIN CHOCOLATE CAKE
7 teaspoons of baking soda. 2 cups flour. 4 kracked eggs. Frosting. 3 cups kockonut. Bake for 1 hour.

PIG IN A BLACKE
You need Backn, chess, hot dog. Take the hot dog. Rap the chess around the hot dog. Put the Backn on top. Cook for 10 minits on Broll. Tron over. Surv.

HAMBGRS
Bie some hambgr mete. Smash the hambgr mete. Put some solt on the hambgrs. Put in oven at 509 tempchr. Cuk four 2 days.

LIMMINADE
Get a Limmin out and get a can and SCWEASE hard. Poot it in the ferig.

COOKIES!!!
4 tablespoons of baking soda, 2 teaspoons of salt. Mix well. Bake to 35 degress for 3 hours. Add 2 eggs, 4 cups of flour. Mix tell know lumps. Then bake to 35 degrees for two hours. Then take out and let cool. THEN EAT!!!

RICE KRIPIES CAKE

2 cups rice kripies—1 half bar butter—1 jar marshmellow cream. Put 1 cup pepper, 2 tablespoons of sugar, a dap of salt. Let butter melt at 300 F. put in rice kripies. Add marshmellow creme. Stir for 1 hour. Put in pan in oven and set time for 24 hours. Its super. Try it!

SPAGHETTI

Put a pot of hot water on and let it boil for a half an hour then put the spaghetti in the pot for 10 minets then drain the water and put the spaghetti in a bull.

GARLIC TOAST

Put a tablespoon of garlic on bread and put it in the oven for 20 minuts at 200 degrees.

HAMBURGER

Wad with hands into patties. Cook in oven 70 degress for 20 hours. If they aren't done, set the timer for another 20 hours. Put on buns. Good with mustard and catsup.

CANDY

You get some food coler and you get a cooky cuter and you put them in the fricer and there you are.

PIZZA

You take crust then you take doe then you rubbit then you put cheez on top then you bake it.

SURPRISE COOKIES: YUM YUM

1 eggs. 2 cups sugar, ½ cup flour, 1 teaspoon of water, 3 tablespoons of powered sugar, ½ sticks of butter. Note. Mix together good. Rool with a rooling pen. Thin cut it in half.

Use one half and cut into 3 inch squares. Put rasands or gumdrops or anythings you wish. Put in oven for 8 minutes for good ones. Good luck.

SORR CRM PANCAKES
Sorr crm—1 cup flore—1 cup Srupe—cook for 5 mines tempuchr 150. Then srve.

HAMBAGERS
Mama puts the hambager in her hand and she flatens it out. And cooks it to 301 degrexe. When it done she puts musturd and ketchup and then I eat it. And sometimes I ask for another one.

TACOS
Put in 2 millemeters of meat and 2 tablespoons and one cup of lettus and 2 cups of cheese and some hot Sues.

PIZZA
Get a roll of dough and roll into a circle. ½ cup of tonanto sause, 3 pound of cheese, 1 pound of hambeger, 3 cups of caiton bacon. Sprikle the sause on the crust then put the cheese on then the hambeger, then the caiton bacon. Cook at 300 put the pizza in carefully. Cook for 30 mintis and voila, its done!

ASPAIRGIS
Frist you wash it off then you cook it.

CHOCLIT CAKE WITH CHOCLIT FROSTING
Fix it. Bake it. Eat it.

I don't know who wrote those last two recipes, but I'd be willing to bet it was somebody related to me.

14

History vs. Herstory

Now I know why they call it *"history."* Nobody ever asked for *her* story.

What is history, anyway, except one guy's version of a current event, which has acquired credibility simply by appearing in print? The older the story gets, the more unquestionable it becomes; should it eventually appear in the history books, credibility evolves into infallibility.

But what if the guy got the facts wrong in the first place? Just think about "history." We swallow all that stuff about ancient Greece and the Gallic wars and the Roosevelt administrations, never for a minute wondering if there might have been another side to the story. (Like *her* side.)

The longer I live the more I wonder about the accuracy of

history. We accept this story from a guy who probably wasn't even there. Most likely he based the story on bits and pieces he picked up from the neighbors, or worse, from somebody's kids. I shudder when I think of the reliability of such sources.

Take, for example, a story that appeared in this morning's paper, headlined: FIRE RAGES OUT OF CONTROL AS MOTHER BEATS HELPLESS CHILD. An accompanying picture might verify the facts: firemen rushing around wearing those big helmets and dragging those big hoses, while in the foreground an unidentified fireman seems to be trying to restrain a woman whose child is cowering on the ground.

I didn't read the story because I knew the story. I was there.

It was not "a raging fire." It was a little smoke coming from our charcoal grill which poofed a few sparks when I squirted a little kerosene on the coals. Okay, so maybe it was more than a little kerosene, and the sparks could have looked like flames, but I had everything under control. There was really no reason for the neighbors to call the fire department, or for the fire dispatcher to notify the newspapers. No one was more surprised than I when I heard sirens coming from two directions (do they always send a rescue squad with the fire trucks?) and watched firemen descend on my back yard wielding axes and dragging eighty feet of firehose across my newly seeded lawn, followed by a news photographer with three cameras hanging around his neck. I suppose I shouldn't have lost my temper and shouted at them. Certainly, if I had known that my picture was going to be all over the morning papers, I wouldn't have picked that particular moment to take a swat at my seventeen-year-old son who wandered on the scene and asked: "When are we gonna eat?"

Now really, doesn't that make you wonder?

Consider the French Revolution. Has it ever occurred to anybody that maybe Marie Antoinette was just a misunderstood housewife who spent an entire afternoon baking cookies and cakes for the peasants, only to have those ingrates come around and tell her they'd rather eat bread?

Just think of the possibilities of herstory. Surely history students who have struggled through Schlesinger and White would rather read *Inside Camelot* by Jacqueline Kennedy, or even Ethel. If Winston Churchill's *Finest Hours* made the best-seller lists, think what a book blitz Clementine could have caused had she written of Churchill's *Happy Hours!* And what one of us would not love to see those Roosevelt biographers get put in their place by one last word from Eleanor. I know, she wrote her autobiography *This I Remember . . .* would that she could come back long enough to write a sequel: *This I Forgot.*

The truth is, women see life differently than men do.

I realized this one evening some years ago when I attended a party for our newly elected congressman and his wife. In the ladies' room before dinner I overheard the congressman's wife talking about her first visit to the White House.

"It was glorious!" she said enthusiastically. "It was a warm night, but, fortunately, there was a gentle rain falling, so we weren't sweltering while we were standing in line to get into the White House. Guess who was right behind us? Ted and Joan Kennedy! And the Howard Bakers were in front of us. So many celebrities! We all got to shake hands with the President and First Lady, and then we went into the dining room where we were served the most scrumptious banquet: coq au vin beaujolais, petits pois à la almondine, tangerines vouvray . . . it was superb! But the best part of the evening was the entertainment: Pablo Casals, the famous cellist! It was fantastic!"

An hour later, I overheard the congressman describing the same event.

"God, what a night!" he said. "It was awful. We had to

stand in line in this pouring rain, squeezed between Teddy Kennedy and Howard Baker who kept throwing barbs back and forth about some boring bill, while their wives stood there looking at each other as if to say: 'And people wonder why!' It took so long to get through the damned receiving line we didn't even get a drink before dinner . . . if you can call it dinner. Chicken stew, nutty peas, and sour oranges. Then to add insult to injury, we had to spend the next two hours in the East Room listening to some guy play the fiddle. And to think I could have been home watching the football game! What a fiasco!"

I'm not saying his story wasn't accurate; I'm just saying that if I was teaching sixth-grade social studies, I'd opt for *her* story.

Another historical event which should have been herstorical was the Blizzard of '75. We in the Midwest tend to call every gusty snowstorm a blizzard but, actually, we seldom see more than one real blizzard in a lifetime. I have seen my real blizzard.

On January 10, 1975, we in Omaha awoke to a snowstorm that was soon to bear all the marks of a true blizzard: heavy snow, subzero temperatures, wild winds, and deep drifts. Traffic was at a standstill; everything was shut down, including the schools . . . a fact which drove mothers wild, as we had not yet recovered from the "togetherness" of Christmas vacation.

Ordinarily, I keep our pantry full of food, but during the holidays our kids had outeaten themselves. Consequently, I had to spend the next five days snowbound with ten kids, two dogs, four jars of peanut butter, one bottle of catsup, and sixteen almost-empty boxes of dry cereal.

Where was my husband? He went to work, of course. I know, the streets were impassable; he couldn't drive. But he took one look at the kids, the dogs, the wild-eyed wife, and concluded that he would rather battle the elements than the offspring. I didn't blame him for risking life and limb to get to his quiet, peaceful office, with its goody-filled vending machines, its library full of reading material, its proximity to a bar across the way. What I blamed him for was not taking me with him.

It was, to put it kindly, a memorable week. While the winds howled outside, the kids howled inside. They argued, they fought, they wrestled and rolled; they drove their mother wild. I suggested they play Monopoly. They said the pieces were missing. I suggested they sit around the fire and sing songs; the fire wouldn't start and the songs were unsingable. Now I know why their generation finds it necessary to freak out on funny cigarettes during those four-hour concerts. It's the only way they can stand the music. Not to mention each other.

I couldn't even send them outside to shovel the driveway, because we couldn't find the shovels. Somebody had left them lying under sixteen inches of snow.

By the fourth day, the kids were so goofy they were doing algebra assignments, and I was so hyper I holed myself up in the basement and did all the ironing. That's how close I was to hysteria. Is cabin fever ever fatal?

All this time, of course, Himself was lazing around his office, munching candy bars, reading magazines, and trekking across the street for beer and roast beef. We talked on the phone several times a day, and while he assured me he was catching up on a lot of work, I suspect he spent most of the day working crossword puzzles and writing letters. In fact, my mother showed me a letter he wrote to her during that blizzard, verifying my belief that *his* story is never quite like *her* story. It read:

"Dear Mrs. Burrowes:

Just a note to let you know all is well here, in spite of the weather, which isn't as bad as news reports would have you believe. I don't know why they closed the schools; in my day we walked through drifts twice this deep. Teresa and the kids are safe and snug at home probably playing a Monopoly marathon, or making big batches of fudge. How I envy them! I felt it was necessary for me to come to the office, and now it seems I am stranded here. But don't worry about me; there are candy bars in the vending machine (a little stale, but I'll offer it up) and I can, if necessary, force myself to eat those awful sandwiches from that sleazy bar across the street. I just talked to Teresa on the phone; it sounds like they are having a ball! The kids were making jolly sounds in the background, and Teresa was laughing so hard it sounded as if she were crying. How I wish I were there!

Love,
Lee."

In some cases I am relieved to note that his-story is more accurate than her-story. Such was the case the night our son John wrecked my car. Fortunately, nobody was injured, which was miraculous when you consider the damage to the car and the fact that it was filled with eighth-grade girls.

John had reluctantly agreed to chauffeur his little sister and her friends to cheerleading practice at the grade school, and just after he had picked up the last cheerleader, he pulled out into a busy thoroughfare and was hit broadside by another car. In spite of the terrible impact, and the subsequent shock, all of the passengers had total recall.

John's version: "I had stopped for the red light; all the girls were giggling and jumping around, and Mary was yakking

away as usual but I wasn't paying any attention to them. . . .
I was just waiting for the light to change. When it turned
green, I looked both ways, didn't see anybody, pulled out into
the intersection, and WHAMMO! I hadn't seen the guy because he didn't have his lights on; he admitted that; he said
he didn't realize how dark it had gotten. Don't ask me why he
was sailing through a red light. I'm sorry about the damage to
the car; it wouldn't have been so bad except that I lost control
and swerved into a tree. I guess I was so concerned about
those kids, I wasn't thinking about what else I might hit."

His sister's version: "He was showing off for my friends
and I kept telling him to WATCH WHERE YOU'RE
GOING; SLOW DOWN; TURN HERE; NO NOT
HERE, HERE!; WATCH THE LIGHT, IT'S GREEN,
DUMMY; HURRY UP OR WE'LL BE LATE; BE CARE-
FUL! but he wouldn't listen to me. Why doesn't he ever lis-
ten to me?"

Blonde cheerleader's version: "It was just awful! I mean, it
was really wild, you know? Wow, I mean it was rea-ee-lly
bad. I just can't bear to even think about it. My favorite pom-
pom got smashed!"

Brunette cheerleader's version: "It wasn't John's fault; he
was just wonderful. You were so good, John! I wasn't a bit
scared or hurt or anything. John was so brave; he was just
wonderful. Honest. Say, John . . . don't you think an eighth-
grade girl who is almost fourteen years old should be allowed
to date?"

Redhead cheerleader's version: "Accident? What accident?
Don't you remember? I wasn't there! I was taking my piano
lesson! Oh, my mother's gonna kill me!"

The more I consider history, the more I become convinced
that our country should have a primary historian . . . sort of
a poet laureate with pay. Otherwise we will continue to have
conflicting and confusing versions of every event. For exam-

ple, wouldn't you hate to be a history student a generation
from now, trying to understand the Kennedy years, after
reading Schlesinger's account, and then Victor Lasky's? And
what of Watergate? Whose version do you believe? Wood-
ward and Bernstein's? Haldeman's? Jaworsky's? John
Dean's? President Nixon's? . . . or Art Buchwald?

There you go! The perfect compromise. From henceforth it
shall be neither *history* nor *herstory*, but *theirstory*. I can see
it now: *A Comprehensive Study of Twentieth-Century
America* by Buchwald and Bloomingdale.

I'd believe it; wouldn't you?

15

Would Somebody Call Me a Taxi, Please?

June 15, 1975

Ms. June Welty, Assistant Manager
Family Insurance Department
Alexander and Alexander Inc.
Omaha, Nebraska

Dear Ms. Welty:

This is to inform you that we recently purchased a second car and we will need to have our policy revised to cover our four teenage sons: Lee, John, Michael, and James. Thank you so much.

Sincerely,
Mrs. A. Lee Bloomingdale (Teresa)

June 25, 1975

Ms. June Welty, Family Insurance Department
Alexander and Alexander Inc.
Omaha, Nebraska

Dear Ms. Welty:
I just received the first premium notice on our revised auto policy, and I have one question: ARE YOU KIDDING? I realize that unmarried males under the age of 25 raise the premium somewhat, but this is ridiculous.
Please explain.

Sincerely,
Mrs. A. Lee Bloomingdale (Teresa)

July 3, 1975

Ms. June Welty, Family Insurance Dept.
Alexander and Alexander Inc.
Omaha, NE.

Dear Ms. Welty:
Oh. I didn't realize that accidents or traffic violations could raise premium payments so much, and truly I had forgotten that all four boys have had accidents this past year, and three of them were ticketed. (A mother tries to forget these little things.) My check will be in the mail as soon as our second mortgage goes through.

Gratefully,
Mrs. Lee Bloomingdale (Teresa)

September 16, 1975

June Welty, FID
Alexander and Alexander Inc.
Omaha, NE.

Dear Ms. Welty:

This is to inform you that our son Lee had a slight mishap
with our car last night. Estimates of damages will be sent to
you by all four parties involved. The accident report will be
filed just as soon as Lee can satisfactorily explain how he
managed to hit three cars and a truck, all parked in the same
lot.

Sincerely,
Mrs. Lee Bloomingdale (Teresa)

January 9, 1976

June Welty
A and A Inc.
Omaha, NE.

Dear June:

I regret to report that during last night's heavy rainstorm a
fire hydrant got in the way of my car while our son John was
driving. There was no damage to the car, but the city would
like to be reimbursed for the fire hydrant. A bill will be forth-
coming.

Sincerely,
Teresa Bloomingdale (Mrs. A. Lee Bloomingdale)

April 16, 1976

Dear June Welty:

Here's another one. Sorry about that. Mike says he did, too, look both ways and the motorcycle "just came out of nowhere." Fortunately, the motorcycle rider was not injured. Unfortunately, the motorcycle rider was a policeman. Will that make a difference on our premium?

Sincerely,
Teresa Bloomingdale

June 10, 1976

Dear June:

This is to inform you that our son Lee has moved to South Dakota. As he is no longer in residence here, please remove him from our auto policy. Will there be a refund on our last premium?

Sincerely,
Teresa

July 5, 1976

Dear June:

I am returning the refund on our last premium as partial payment for the increase on our next premium, due to Jim's accident of the 28th. Please lower our deductible to $100 and increase our liability to one million dollars. Thanks so much.

Nervously,
Teresa

September 4, 1976

Dear June:

This is to inform you that our son John will be moving to Lincoln on Monday and can therefore be removed from our auto policy.

Sincerely,
Teresa

January 2, 1977

Dear June:

In regard to the New Year's Eve accident I called you about this morning, I cannot send a full report until Mike and Jim remember which of them was driving, and just what it was they ran into.

Have a Happy New Year.

Teresa

March 19, 1977

Dear June:

Please add our daughter Mary to our auto policy. I understand she will get a discount, as she is a nonsmoker.

Sincerely,
Teresa

April 11, 1977

Dear June:
Does our auto policy cover fire damage to the car's interior?
Please remove Mary's discount as a nonsmoker.

Sincerely,
Teresa

September 2, 1977

Dear June:
Please reinstate Lee on our auto policy, as he has moved
back home. Please remove Mike from our auto policy, as he
has gone away to college.

Thanks,
Teresa

December 1, 1977

Dear June:
Please remove our son Lee from our auto policy, as he got
married. Please reinstate our son John as he has moved back
home.
I hope this doesn't confuse you as much as it does me.

Sincerely,
Teresa

March 15, 1978

Dear June:

Please remove our son Jim from our auto policy, as he has enlisted in the Marines. (He was assigned to the Motor Pool; I wonder what the Marines pay in premiums?)

Optimistically,
Teresa

October 1, 1978

Dear June:

Thank you for revising our policy to include our son Dan. Enclosed are estimates of the damage done to both of our cars when Dan backed the station wagon out of the garage and rammed into the sedan.

Will our premiums go up if the Number One driver of the station wagon goes on tranquilizers?

Pessimistically,
Teresa

January 7, 1979

Dear June:

This is to request another revision on our policy. Our son John has moved into his own apartment, and can thus be removed from our policy.

His brother Michael has moved back home, and must thus be reinstated on our policy.

Would it be possible to double our liability while Jim is home on leave? (If they would put a Marine behind the wheel of every military vehicle, we wouldn't need nuclear weapons to intimidate the enemy.)

Sincerely,
Teresa

P.S. Mary wants to know if she gets a driver's discount as she hasn't been behind the wheel in over 12 months.

December 29, 1979

Dear June:

There is good news and there is bad news.

The good news is: Mike is moving into his own apartment, and thus joins his three brothers in being *off* our auto insurance policy.

The bad news is: The night before he moved out, Mike totaled my car.

Estimates are enclosed. Please make the check payable to me, personally, so I can endorse it over to the bicycle shop. Is it true that you never forget how to ride a bike?

Sincerely,
Teresa

"Hello, Alexander and Alexander? This is A. Lee Bloomingdale. May I speak to June Welty, please? . . . June, Lee Bloomingdale. I'm surprising Teresa with a new car, and we'll need full coverage on it, as the kids will be driving it. There will be Mary and Dan, of course, and Peg, too, as she will get her license this month. Will Ann need to be on when she gets her Learner's Permit? No need to worry about Tim or Pat just yet. And while I've got you on the phone, June, our son John called me the other day and asked me if you could handle his motorcycle insurance. Will you take care of all that for me, June? . . . June? . . . June? Are you there, June? Hello? . . ."

16

No Time to Divorce

When people ask my husband and me how we have managed to hold our marriage together for lo these many years (on July second next we will have been married forever), we admit we probably would have been divorced any number of times had it not been for one important factor: interruptions.

Every time we would get into a rip-roarin' fight, one or the other of the kids would fall off a trike, or come down with tonsilitis, or throw up all over the car, and by the time we got the skinned knee kissed, the tonsils removed, or the car cleaned up, we would have forgotten what it was we were arguing about.

Of course, that isn't the only thing that has held our marriage together. There has also been love, loyalty, the knowledge that my mother would kill me if I ever so much as considered deserting her beloved son-in-law, and that greatest of all divorce deterrents: the question of Custody of the Children. With ten kids, you don't take that matter lightly, let me tell you. While I have no doubt that my husband would insist that I get the children (and I would be equally adamant that he be so blessed), there is another problem involved. In these modern courts, all too often the judge leaves the question of custody up to the kids themselves. Both my husband and I cringe at the thought of our children sitting in a courtroom full of scribbling journalists, weighing the pros and cons of Mom versus Dad, emphatically embellishing the cons. The neighbors know enough about us, thank you. I'm not about to have our cons spread all over the evening newspaper.

I suppose that's why so many couples wait until their kids are grown up and gone before they file for divorce, but isn't that silly? If your kids are grown up and gone, why would you need a divorce?

Frankly, I have never been able to understand why couples who have made it through two decades of marriage can't finish the course. Surely by that time she has adjusted to his snoring and eating crackers in bed, and he must be resigned to her refusal to cook hominy grits or iron pajamas. Yet you see it all the time: couples in their fifties, sixties, even seventies are splitting up and going their separate ways.

Just the other night my husband came home from the office and told me he had heard good friends of ours are getting divorced.

"I can't believe that!" I said. "It's just not possible! Why would a nice guy like Jed walk out on that sweet wife of his? And after all these years?"

"It seems that ol' Jed got himself a girlfriend," said my husband, "and he wants to marry her."

"Why?" asked our college-age son with all the logic of the modern male.

"Some people *do* think marriage is the way to go," said his father, "strange as that may seem to one of your generation."

"It seems strange to one of *my* generation," I said, "that a man who has been married for twenty-five years, who has seen his kids through the toddler years, the trauma of grade school, and the terrible teens, would want to run the risk of starting all over again. How old is his lady friend, anyway?"

"Twenty-five, I think," said my husband.

"Good lord!" I said. "Jed really is starting all over again! What a horrible thought!"

"What I can't understand is: how does a guy that old attract a girl half his age? No sexy young gals ever flirt with me!" said my husband.

"Well you don't have to sound so sad about it," I said. "Anyway, what makes you think the women inaugurate those affairs? I bet the men are responsible for a lot of the flirting and fooling around."

"Really?" asked my husband in genuine surprise. "Where do you suppose they find the time for that sort of thing?"

"Where do you suppose they find the *money* for that sort of thing?" I asked with a laugh. "One nice thing about having this expensive big family is you couldn't woo a girl if you wanted to!"

"What would you do if Daddy ever did get a girlfriend, Mom?" asked Tim as he helped me with the supper dishes.

"I'd tell him to bring her home so she could take her turn at the dishes," I told Tim, with a reassuring hug. Do kids really worry about those things? Evidently they do, for Annie asked in horror:

"Wouldn't it be awful if Daddy had an affair?"

"Don't worry about it, kiddo," said her big brother Dan. "It will never happen."

"What makes you so sure?" asked Annie.

"Because I know Dad," said Dan. "If Dad ever wanted to ask a girl for a date, he would make Mom call her; he'd make me pick her up and take her home; he'd insist on seeing her here because you know darn well he hates to go out; and they sure couldn't get anything done here 'cause you little kids would always be interrupting!"

Didn't I tell you? Interruptions have saved many a marriage!

What really saves marriages, however, is learning to avoid all those pitfalls which cause so much friction between husband and wife. Unfortunately, young marrieds don't learn about these pitfalls until they have already fallen into the pit. As one who has become an expert on pitfalls, I would like to offer here a list of Things a Husband and Wife Should Never Do Together.

1. *Take a shower.* This idiotic idea was thought up by some movie director who needed an R rating. (How they ever got the picture finished, I'll never know; the costars had surely stopped speaking to each other after the first take.) There are all kinds of problems involved with two people taking a shower together, not the least of which is the size of the shower. I have never seen a shower big enough to hold two filthy children, let alone two frolicking adults. What do you do if she likes it hot and he wants it cold? Or he prefers spout and she favors spray? And who gets first dibs on the soap? (Who gets out of the shower to get a new bar if there isn't any soap in the shower in the first place?) And who has to bend over to pick up the soap when it gets dropped down into the drain? (She does, I'll bet.) Frankly, I can't imagine anything more detrimental to a marriage than sharing a shower.

2. *Shop for groceries.* Now I know that a lot of young wives want their husbands along when shopping for groceries

so that he can see how expensive everything is and how impossible it is for her to keep within their grocery budget. Of course she can't keep within the budget if she lets him tag along! There isn't a husband alive who can walk through a grocery store with his hands in his pockets. They are like little kids in the cereal section, grabbing for all the goodies . . . only their specialty is "gourmet." While his wife is pawing over lettuce and cucumbers, hubby is packing in anchovies and avocados. She can, of course, insist that he stay with her "to offer advice," but his advice will cost her money, for while she muses over the meat counter, considering the various types of hamburger, he will be arguing the merits of sirloin steak. When she picks up two loaves of bread, he will sneak a dozen doughnuts and six cupcakes into the basket, and if she pushes that basket past the candy counter, she's had it. No, wifey; never take a husband to the grocery store.

3. *Punish a child.* I know the modern theory is for parents to sit in judgment together, the idea being, I suppose, for the kid to realize he hasn't got a chance, it being two against one. But I have found that if my husband and I attempt to punish a child together, the only one who comes out unscathed is the child. The problem is, I think, that fathers believe in physical punishment ("let's give the kid a swat and get it over with") while mothers prefer the verbal approach (yelling), which always gets to Dad before it bothers the kid. If Dad can be coerced into forgoing the swat, he will invariably insist on "Okay, you're grounded for a week!"—an edict which inspires Mom to shout: "Oh no he's not; you don't have to stay home all day and put up with him!" The ideal situation would be for Mom and Dad to sit down beforehand and discuss the matter sensibly and quietly so that there won't be any contradictions or criticisms when the punishment is finally carried out. The kids like this idea because they know

very well that by the time Mom and Dad get to sit down and discuss anything, the whole episode will probably be long forgotten. Frankly, I have always felt it was something of a mortal sin for a mother to threaten: "Just wait till your father comes home; you'll really get it!" It may terrorize the kid, but it's not fair to the father. If it's the "agony of anticipation" she wants to invoke, she can say, "I'm going to punish you, just as soon as I can think up something horrible enough!" She may never be able to think up anything very horrible, but believe me, the kid will, and just dwelling on it will be punishment enough.

4. *Clean closets, cabinets, the attic, et cetera.*   If you insist on cleaning closets, cabinets, et cetera (fortunately, modern married couples are learning how to put off this task indefinitely, if not permanently), assign his and hers cabinets and never watch what the other is discarding. He will want to save everything she throws away, and she cannot do without those things he calls trash. Awful arguments can ensue over such ridiculous items as his fraternity beer mugs or such cherished treasures as her high school prom program. Better to leave everything as is, and when the closets and cabinets get too crowded, move.

5. *Look for a pair of pliers.*   Husbands metamorphose when they start searching for their pliers. Even before opening the tool chest, they assume (usually correctly) that the pliers will be missing. The most gentle of husbands turns into a raving madman the moment his pliers take a powder, and accusations are always thrown at the nearest suspect who, for some dumb reason, feels obligated to help her husband in the search. The wife often makes matters worse by issuing denials that she took his precious pliers, and may even instigate divorce proceedings by suggesting that perhaps he did not put the pliers away after he used them yesterday out on the back

porch. (If the pliers are, in fact, found on the back porch, she's all through.) The solution here is to let him look for the darn pliers all by himself, then when he finds them he can lie about it and claim they were in the kitchen drawer where she "undoubtedly put them and just forgot."

"I guess I shouldn't be so surprised about Jed's divorce," I told my husband the other night as we were getting ready for bed. 'I saw them at the supermarket not long ago; she was complaining that he kept loading up the basket with gourmet goodies, and he was complaining because he had to buy a new pliers since she has lost his again."

"It wasn't the pliers that did it," my husband reminded me. "It was that peach in his office."

"How is his wife taking it?" I asked. "Has anybody heard?"

"Very well, I presume," said my husband, "since she just left for the Bahamas with the lawyer who handled the divorce. I understand they are going to get married."

"I give up!" I said. "My peers never cease to astound me! Can you imagine breaking in a new spouse, at their age? I'm glad I don't have to start all over again; I don't even have the energy for another honeymoon!"

"Wanna bet?" leered my lover, as he switched out the light.

Then, of course, there are some positive aspects in holding a marriage together. . . .

17

What's for

Dinner, Mrs. Skinner?

"Lee wants me to get your recipe for baked beans," my daughter-in-law, Karen, said over the phone. "He says your baked beans are terrific and mine are terrible. I can't understand it, because I followed the recipe in that cookbook you gave me. Do you have some special secret for cooking baked beans?"

"Special secret?" I stalled. Should I tell her? I know it's tradition that cooks never confide their culinary secrets, but what the heck? Karen is family! Furthermore, if my son is not satisfied with what is served at *her* table, he just may start reappearing at *mine*.

"I'll give you my recipe for baked beans, Karen," I told her, "if you promise not to tell anyone."

"Oh, I promise!" she said. "Just let me get a pencil so I can write this down."

"I don't think you'll need to write it down," I told her. "The recipe is fairly simple."

"Good!" she said. "I'm not into gourmet cooking."

"I'm glad to hear that, dear," I told her. "You and I are going to get along famously. Here's the baked-bean recipe. Take one can of pork and beans; pour into pan; heat and eat."

"That's it?" she asked in surprise. "You mean that's all there is to it? You just heat up a can of plain old pork and beans? No molasses? No spices? No special sauces?"

"Sometimes I dump a little catsup in it," I admitted.

"I don't believe this!" she laughed. "When I think of the hours I spent, soaking those darn beans, and measuring ingredients, and baking and rebaking. No wonder Lee thought they were "terrible"; they didn't taste like canned beans. Incidentally, he wants me to get your recipe for spinach, too. Is it the same as the one for baked beans?"

"Of course not, Karen," I said. "Whoever heard of putting catsup on spinach? Try vinegar, instead."

"I love this!" said Karen. "You make cooking so easy!"

"Sshhh! That's the part that's secret!" I told her. "Never let your husband know how easy cooking can be unless, of course, you intend to try to persuade him to take his turn in the kitchen. I wouldn't advise it, however. He can't cook anything but pissghetti."

"But WHAT?" she asked.

"Spaghetti," I amended quickly. "The kids have called it pissghetti for so long I forgot its real name . . . though I don't know how I could forget it. That's the only thing I cook that they really like."

Contrary to what my children would have you believe, I am not a lousy cook, nor am I a lazy one. I put a great deal of time and effort into choosing the very best canned vegetables, the finest frozen entrees, the tastiest takeout dinners. Sometimes I even jazz up a recipe with a gourmet touch of my own: an extra egg in the cake mix; more cheese in the au gratin casserole; a cup of wine in the beef stew. Though I did learn that the stew tastes better if you put the wine in first. (Not in the stew. In you.)

I first became aware of my culinary deficiencies when, as a young bride, I cooked my first roast and came face to face with the *bête noire* of every chef: gravy.

"Gravy is easy," my mother had told me. "You just remove the roast from the pan, skim the fat off the drippings, stir in a little warm water and a little flour, and there you have it: delicious brown gravy."

There *she* may have delicious brown gravy; what *I* have there is scorched starch.

I have been attempting gravy for twenty-five years, and you would think by now I would realize that the very recipe indicates it is impossible. The first clue is "Remove the roast from the pan." How? I can never get the darn meat out of the pan; it is always either stuck solid, or it is floating in the drippings and when I lift the meat from pan to platter I drip juices all over the floor. (Do you suppose that's why they're called "drippings"?)

And how does one "skim the fat off the drippings"? With a spoon? A syringe? Neither works. There is only one infallible method and that is to put the whole pan in the refrigerator and leave it there until the fat congeals enough to be lifted off. Of course, this tends to prolong the cocktail hour, but that's all right. If your guests drink enough martinis they won't notice that the roast is cold.

Once the fat is removed, it must be reheated, as some of it must be readded to the drippings. You then add warm water and flour, stirring till the gravy is smooth, which it will be after you scoop out, one by one, the 9,674 lumps that formed because you didn't stir fast enough.

Once the lumps are removed and the gravy reheated, you put it on a back burner to get it out of the way while you carve the roast. Then, just before you serve the guests, open a can of beef gravy, heat, and serve with the roast.

What do you do with the stuff sitting on the back burner? Store it in the refrigerator. It will come in handy when you want to patch the cracks in your son's bedroom walls.

A simpler recipe, though one avoided by all cooks, is the recipe for white sauce. White sauce is easier than brown gravy because in white sauce there is no roast to be removed, no fat to be skimmed, no drippings to drip. Just melt a little butter, stir in some flour, add a little milk, and I guarantee that you'll have just as many lumps as gravy, but with a lot less work. Furthermore, the white sauce blends a lot better with most bedroom decors.

My failures with gravy and sauces are exceeded only by my failure with gelatin. I have, on a couple of occasions, made suitable sauces, but I have *never* made edible gelatin, though I follow directions faithfully.

"Dissolve powder in hot water; add cold water, stir until slightly thickened, chill until set." Doesn't that sound simple? How could anybody botch that up? I'll tell you how. If the water isn't hot enough, the powder won't dissolve; if the water isn't cold enough, the gelatin won't set. (Add too much water, and you get Kool-Aid.) I finally found the perfect formula for getting the gelatin to set. Dissolve the powder in *boiling* water, then quickly stir in *ice cubes*. The gelatin will set perfectly. Of course, you can't eat it; it's full of shattered glass.

If there is anything I dread more than following a recipe, it is making up a menu. I know there are all kinds of books featuring menus for everyday and every occasion, as well as a multitude of magazines offering delectable dishes to please every palate. But I never seem to have the ingredients called for: "Ground arrowroot" . . . "6 qts. of pea pods" . . . "fresh fennel seeds" . . . "Breast of spring lamb" . . . and here I am with a freezerful of fall lamb.

Why don't recipes ever call for those things I always seem to have on hand? "Half a cup of last Tuesday's green pea soup?" (Or maybe that's the Tuesday before last's cream of chicken soup.) . . . "a half a bottle of catsup?" (a whole bottle of ketchup? . . . a smidgen left in the bottle of catchup?) . . . "twelve opened cans of fruit cocktail" (takes that many to get enough cherries) . . . "one bitten-into apple" . . . "four containers of scorched starch" . . . ?

And I am certainly not interested in yet one more way to cook hamburger. I haven't perfected the first way yet. I want suggestions that are exciting, exotic, and cheap. Most important, I want menus that are suggested by somebody else.

Last Sunday I was dreading another week of dinner-decisions when I read in Heloise's helpful-hints column a letter from a housewife who claimed she has no trouble planning meals, she just lets her family take turns choosing the daily menus. Can you imagine that? Neither can I, but I'll try anything once.

On Monday morning, therefore, I asked my husband what he would like for dinner that evening.

"I don't care," he said, as he has every morning for the past twenty-five years. "Anything will be fine." So . . . I cooked Anything, and he had had it for lunch.

The next morning I asked Tim and Patrick to choose the supper menu.

"You mean we can have anything we want?" they asked enthusiastically.

"That's right," I replied recklessly. "You name it and I'll serve it."

"Ice cream sundaes!" said Tim.

"With chocolate nut brownies!" added Patrick.

We compromised; they got cookies and ice cream, but only after they ate all their meat loaf.

Wednesday was the girls' day to choose. After a lengthy period of contemplation, Ann announced she wanted bistecca alla pizzaiola, Peggy preferred coq au vin rouge, and Mary suggested quiche de George de Fessenheim. Show-offs! That's what I get for letting my daughters bum around restaurants reading menus.

I had to admit their suggestions were exotic enough, but I wasn't about to cook any of them as that would mean breaking my hard-fast kitchen rule never to cook anything I can't spell or pronounce. So we had pissghetti.

On Thursday the older boys needed no time at all to suggest their favorite menu: "McDonald's!"

One tends to think of McDonald's as an economical place to eat. This may be true for the average family with 1.8 children, but for those of us who are raising an entire football team, an order from McDonald's can cost a small fortune. But what the heck? It's only money! On to the Golden Arches!

I'll say this for the kids who take the orders at McDonald's: nothing phases them. When I gave my order for twelve plain hamburgers, eight Big Macs, four cheeseburgers, four french-fried potatoes, six french-fried onions, and twelve chocolate shakes, the young lady wrote it all down, looked at me standing there all alone, and asked politely: "To go?"

I resisted the temptation to tell her No, I'd eat it there.

On Friday night we had noodles Budapest, because that was Mrs. Skinner's recipe for the week. My kids always know what to expect for Friday night supper; they simply stop by the store on the way home from school and read the current recipe on the "What's for Dinner, Mrs. Skinner?" pasta package.

On Saturday night, Lee and Karen were coming for dinner, so I called Karen and asked her to choose the menu.

"How about some of your delicious fried chicken?" she suggested. "Lee loves it, and so do I. And since we'll be driving to your house, we could stop by the Colonel's and pick it up for you."

That's what I love about Karen; she's a quick learner.

18

Hello, Dolly!

Before our son married, he and his bride-to-be took a marriage course designed, they concluded, to discourage marriage.

"If we still love each other after that course," he said, "we should love each other the rest of our lives. They didn't leave out a thing."

But, of course, they did. They missed the most controversial domestic problem of all. All they covered were little things like sex and money and how-many-kids, while omitting the problem: Shall we have a dog? I'm here to tell you: If engaged couples were allowed to marry only when and if they agree on the "to have" or "have not" a domestic pet, it just might mean the end of divorce.

As you may have guessed, I am anti-pet. This is not because I am allergic to animals; would that I were. Allergies are socially acceptable; aversions are not, especially aversions to animals beloved by little children and grown men.

Before we got married, my husband and I realized that pets might present a problem, so while it is true that we never got around to discussing such minor matters as whether or not to have children and how many and what sex they should be (how ever do young couples today get anything done, with so many decisions to make?), we did discuss the probability of pets and agreed that for the sake of my sanity, we would shower our affection only on creatures who could follow us into heaven, namely, children.

What both of us failed to realize is: while parents may prefer to shower their affection on children, children prefer to shower their affection on pets. By our fifth wedding anniversary, we had four sons, all of whom would spend half their waking hours running, toddling, or crawling after every four-legged creature in the neighborhood.

"I suppose every little boy should have a dog," said my traitorous husband one Christmas, so I broke down and bought them a dog. Not a real dog, you understand, but a lovely life-like, stuffed collie that looked so much like Lassie my mother once tried to feed it. It was a gorgeous toy, with "real" fur, warm brown-glass eyes, an aristocratic nose, and a long slender body slung low enough for a two-year-old to climb upon and ride. This life-size creature had only one drawback: it terrified our toddlers. They wouldn't touch it.

"That settles it," I told my husband. "If the boys don't like a stuffed dog that doesn't even have teeth, you can imagine how they would take to a live one that bites. Now let's forget about pets."

And we did. Until the boys went to school.

As every parent learns, modern classrooms seldom house such basic items as desks, bookcases, and blackboards. This is not because these things are out of style, but rather because there is no room for them, what with the hamster house, the gerbil wheel, the birdcage, and the aquarium. Instead of learning how to read and write and figure out their allowances, first graders now learn the feeding and breeding of animals, which would be all right with me if the teacher wouldn't draw straws every holiday to see who gets to take the gerbils home, and my kids always got the short straw.

One January I almost got annihilated by twenty-eight angry fourth graders because I had set mousetraps in my basement during the holiday season and had, inadvertently, assassinated their pet gerbil. I might have been more careful had I been aware of the fact that said gerbil was housed in my basement, but my sons had not taken me into their confidence, which is understandable. Had I known that they had hidden a rodent in my basement (they may be called "gerbils" but you and I both know very well, those creatures are just rats in disguise), I would have moved out for the Christmas season and taken the keys to Santa's workshop with me.

That autumn the boys again began to pressure their father for a pet, and he gave them that firm, no-nonsense response that fathers all over the world have been giving their children for generations: "Go ask your mother."

"Why do you *do* that to me?" I asked my husband one night after the kids had exhausted themselves with pet pleas and fallen into bed convinced that their adored father would grant their every wish if it just weren't for mean old Mom.

"We're going to have to give in," my husband said with not-enough reluctance. "Every boy should have a pet. Surely we can find something domesticated enough for you to live with."

"We *have* found something domesticated enough for me to live with," I told him. "Children. Any mother who has potty-trained this many children should not have to concern herself with the bathroom habits of a four-legged creature, and don't give me that old saw about you and the kids taking care of a dog. We all know who would have to take care of a dog, if we had a dog, which we don't."

"We don't have to get a dog," my husband said patiently. "There are all kinds of pets."

"I know that," I told him, "and if you are considering accepting that offer of a free hamster from that cute fourth-grade teacher who keeps ogling you at PTA meetings, you can forget it. I'd let you bring home the teacher before I'd give house room to a hamster."

"How about a cute little kitten?" he suggested.

"Kittens, even the cute ones, have a disgusting habit," I reminded him.

"What's that?" he asked.

"They turn into cats," I replied, "and cats scratch, and claw, and sneak up on you, and shed fur all over your sofa. Forget the cat. Anyway, I thought we agreed to 'no pets allowed' before we got married."

"I know," he said, "but you know how persuasive our kids can be. What would you think about getting them a bird?"

"Not much," I said, "but enough to nix it."

"What have you got against birds?" he asked.

"They tweet," I said. "They tweet when you are on the telephone; they tweet when you're trying to take a nap; they tweet when I'm trying to listen to my Frank Sinatra records. In fact, about the only time they don't tweet is when somebody is trying to get them to show off how well they can tweet. No birds."

"If it's silence you want, how about fish?" he persisted. "Fish don't make any noise, and they are fun to watch."

"Are you kidding?" I asked him. "Have you ever watched fish? They watch you back. In fact they stare at you, all day long. The dumb things never close their eyes. I could never get a thing done if I knew those fish were staring at me all the time."

"A turtle?" he asked weakly, but not yet weak enough.

"Turtles hide," I told him. "My sister had a turtle when we were kids and my mother spent half a summer searching for it, and the other half smelling it because the turtle died someplace in the dining room and we never did find it. Please, no turtles. No pets, period. Didn't we agree years ago that we would not give house room to any creature who could not follow us into heaven?"

"You said it; not I," he sighed.

"Said what?" I asked. (Why do I always ask?)

"We'll just have to get them a pet that can follow them into heaven," he said cheerfully, "a baby sister or brother!"

"Have you ever thought about getting them a dog?" I conceded graciously, though it really didn't make any difference, for by the following summer, our dog Dolly was the first to romp out to the car to greet me as I brought home the new baby, Ann Cecilia.

While I am still anti-animal, I must admit that Dolly was a beautiful creature. A thoroughbred Irish Setter, she was a gentle, aristocratic dog, definitely to the manner born. Unfortunately, she was not also to the manor born; she wouldn't set foot inside our house. I really couldn't blame her. If I had been spoiled by being born in a luxurious, air-conditioned kennel, I would have been reluctant to move into our living quarters, too. I don't know if it was the playpens in our toy-covered living room (only a parent who has two toddlers less than fourteen months apart in age can understand why we needed more than one playpen) or the high chairs in our pablum-splattered kitchen that turned Dolly off, but from the moment she peeked into our domain, she would have none of it. Us she liked; it was the house she hated. (A neighbor suggested that perhaps our house was haunted. How would one know? With everybody claiming that Somebody Else broke the toys, muddied the carpet, slammed the door, or

turned on the TV on a school night, who's to say we didn't
have a ghost?)

So Dolly became our outdoor dog, living year round in our
huge yard, where she spent her days digging and her nights
howling. (The neighbors loved us.) Our yard soon began to
look like those old photographs of the moon: a dreary land-
scape covered with craters. For Dolly, though aristocratic, was
absentminded: she could never remember where her bones
were buried. And like a typical adolescent, she never put back
the dirt.

The digging didn't bother us so much as the howling, for
the digging didn't keep us in almost constant communication
with the neighbors, who would call desperately, in the wee
hours of the morning, to beg us to "take that d— dog inside."

While most people get up in the middle of the night to let
their dog out, we would thus have to get up to let our dog in,
or at least try to get her in, but the mere attempt was usually
all it took to halt the howling. For Dolly was neither hungry
nor unhappy; she was just lonely, and once she had forced
two or three of our kids to come outside and chase her awhile,
she was perfectly content.

If there was anything Dolly enjoyed more than a midnight
romp, it was a midnight snack. For a while we were worried
about Dolly's diet. She turned up her nose at table snacks and
would have little to do with even the most expensive brands
of dog food. Eventually, we figured out why. Dolly preferred
to "dine out." It seems we had some wealthy neighbors who
ate only gourmet food; thus they had gourmet garbage. Dolly,
who could not find a bone she had buried a moment ago,
could sniff out that gourmet garbage the moment the maid
took it out. Before the chateaubriand had cooled in the can,
Dolly would take off (leash, collar, post, and all) for a midnight snack under the stars.

Only once in her lifetime did Dolly deign to come into the house. On the afternoon of May 6, 1975, a terrible tornado destroyed our three-story home. When the warning had sounded, the family had taken shelter in the basement, but we had not had time to unchain Dolly and fight the battle of luring her inside. So when we emerged, unscathed, from our basement refuge, to find our home and the surrounding neighborhood devastated, we were afraid that Dolly had been a victim of that awful wind.

But we found her, wandering dazed and trembling, through the debris of our downstairs, obviously looking for her masters and mistresses. Once she saw us, safe and well, she returned to her outdoor haven, but she would never again dig, or howl, or go out on the town. The noise and violence of that tornado had affected her mentally, and it soon became apparent that she was, after all, a victim. We had to put her to sleep.

I must admit, I miss her, and of course the kids miss her. But you know who misses her most of all? The neighbors.

I'll never understand people.

19

The Rich Scholar

"Hey, Mom," asked our son Dan as he was filling out a questionnaire, "what class are we?"

I thought for a moment. What class?

"Seniors," I said sophomorically. "Or shall we be juniors? Which class has more fun?"

"Aw, Mom, be serious," said Dan. "I gotta know; what class are we? Upper? Middle? Lower?"

"I suppose that would depend on who's doing the classifying," I told him truthfully. "Our uppity neighbor has always been sure we are 'lower,' but your grandmother insists that we are 'upper.' Those who are in-the-know, however, would probably place us in the Great American Middle."

"Who are those in-the-know?" he asked.

"The IRS," I said. "Who else? What are you filling out, anyway?"

"A financial-aid request," he replied. "I'm applying for a college scholarship."

"In that case, go with the neighbors," I said emphatically. "Check 'lower.' And underline it. But do it in pencil; if they think you can afford a pen, they'll shove you into 'upper middle' and tell you to go paddle your own canoe."

I didn't have the heart to tell him he was wasting his time. I know. I have been this route before.

When our first son was preparing for college, he applied for financial aid and was told there should be no problem, as there were over 8,000 various types of scholarships available. That may be true; but what they failed to tell him was, at least 7,975 of them are limited to athletes, and the rest are parceled out to academically superior students who can prove financial need. Since his high school athletics had been pretty much limited to intramural wrestling (the coed variety), he could hardly qualify as an athlete (though he did earn the coveted Octopus award given annually by the Girls Pep Club.) He didn't even try to prove financial need, for he knew he would never be able to prove "academic superiority" with a report card that had seldom seen an A.

Our second son had plenty of A's but he, too, failed to qualify for a scholarship because, despite his close relationship to (as well as often being the cause of) my always in-the-red budget, he could not prove financial need. It seems that eighteen years earlier his godfather had bestowed upon him a small baptismal bequest, which we insisted that he not touch until he went to college. Even with accrued interest, the bequest would barely pay for books and fees, but the Office of Financial Aid considered it a "source of income" and denied him any monetary assistance. (A pronouncement which caused him to cry: "See? I told ya you should have let me buy a motorcycle!")

Oddly enough, had he squandered that bequest on a motorcycle, or even on booze, he might have been eligible for financial aid, as we discovered when our third son (a straight-A student lacking a baptismal bequest or any other source of income) submitted his request for a scholarship. Alas, despite his good grades and indigent status, he too was denied financial aid because he was burdened with an even greater albatross than a baptismal bequest. He had parents.

"What have my parents got to do with this?" he asked the clerk in the Financial Aid Office, where he had been practically camped out all summer, like Lazarus begging for a crumb. "My parents aren't the ones going to college! I am!"

"Yes," replied the clerk, "but we expect parents, whenever possible, to pick up the tab for their children's tuition."

"You just spoke the magic phrase," said my son cheerfully. "When and if it's ever possible, I am sure my parents will gladly fork over the ten grand I will need to get my degree. Right now they have nine other kids, all of whom consider their meals more important than my education."

"I am not responsible for your siblings!" said the clerk firmly (a fact to which I will certainly attest). "Our decision was not based so much on your father's salary as it was on the fact that your family has a savings account."

"We do?" asked our son in surprise. "I didn't know that. Say, how come *you* know that?"

"We have our methods," said the clerk proudly. "In any event, we feel that in light of this cash asset, you do not qualify for financial aid."

When our son related this conversation to me, I couldn't believe it. The next morning I called the Financial Aid Office myself.

"That's correct, Mrs. Bloomingdale," the clerk said in response to my inquiry. "The fact that you have that savings account indicates you can afford to pay your son's tuition."

"Look," I said sincerely, "that savings account isn't really a savings account; it's my station wagon fund. For years I have needed a new station wagon but I cannot afford to pay for a station wagon and finance charges as well, so I have been struggling along with this ten-year-old lemon and in another three hundred dollars I will have my new station wagon. You cannot have my new station wagon!"

"I am sorry," said the clerk, "but rules are rules."

"Am I to understand," I asked with sudden inspiration, "that people who have accumulated any assets are not eligible for aid?"

"That's correct," he said.

"Then how come my neighbor's son got a two-thousand-dollar-grant when his parents own three Cadillacs, a motor launch, and a summer cottage on Cape Cod? Explain that to me!"

"Those are not cash assets," sighed the clerk, "and it is very possible that the vehicles and the cottage are heavily mortgaged."

"So that's the secret!" I said. "Give me thirty minutes. In half an hour I can deplete my cash assets and run up all kinds of bills. Give me till noon, and I can probably even declare bankruptcy!"

The clerk was not amused.

"Tell me," I sighed in resignation, "how did you know about that savings account?"

"Clues!" the clerk admitted proudly. "We learn to spot the clues. In your son's case it was the watch he was wearing the first time he came into this office. There are at least seven hundred students who have one exactly like it. Then there was the pen he used when he filled out the second and third applications. But the clincher was the briefcase he brought in here yesterday. That's when we knew for sure about the savings account."

"But I don't understand," I told him. "What do a watch, a pen, and a briefcase have to do with a savings account?"

"They were premiums!" said the clerk triumphantly. "I recognized those premiums. Frankly, I got one of those briefcases, myself. So you see, I not only know which Savings and Loan you use, I can also make a pretty fair guess as to the amount of the last three deposits!"

"I guess you kids are just going to have to work your way through college," my husband said at dinner that night. "We'll help you all we can, but it looks like 'financial aid' is limited to those who go out for sports, or who belong to a minority group, or who are truly in need."

"Well you won't have to worry about me!" said our eleven-year-old Pat as he wolfed down his third hamburger. "I'm gonna be the star quarterback on the college football team!"

"And you probably won't have to worry about me, either," said Tim, our ninth child, "'cause if Pat keeps eatin' like a pig, by the time I get to college all our money will have gone for food!"

"I think I should qualify under all three categories," offered their sister Mary, who had already completed two years in the university's college of Fine Arts.

"How do you figure that?" asked her brother. "You're not in athletics, you're not in a minority group, and you're not in need."

"Oh, but I am," she said. "I just signed up for Fencing, which is not only considered a sport but which definitely places me in a minority group. There aren't many female fencers, I'll wager!"

"How about the 'need' aspect?" badgered her brother.

"Simple," she said with a sigh. "I've been dating three seniors, all of whom once qualified for that Octopus award. Boy, do I need to know Fencing!"

To our surprise and delight, Dan actually did get a scholarship, but it wasn't based on athletics, social status, or even need. It was, in fact, based on his showing in the American College Tests; he landed in the percentile the examiners refer to as "scholars."

Can you believe that? A scholarship granted to a scholar! What is this country coming to?

20

Off to College

When I went away to college, a generation ago, I took a steamer trunk to hold my clothes and a shopping bag for miscellaneous items such as an alarm clock, an umbrella, a radio, and a tennis racket. I remember my father teasing me about "taking all that stuff to school," and my arguing that these were all "absolute necessities," though I suppose it was a bit much, especially since I was also toting a typewriter, an extra coat, and a huge stuffed animal to which I was not particularly devoted but which was definitely *de rigueur* in a girl's dorm room in that era.

A generation later, when our son John went off to college, things were a bit different. John took a shopping bag to hold his clothes (his entire wardrobe consisting of two pairs of jeans, a couple of T-shirts, and twelve sweat bands) and a U-Haul for his miscellaneous items: refrigerator, recliner, hot plate, sunlamp, television set, full component stereo system, typewriter, tape recorder, ten-speed bike, and numerous boxes of records and books, some of which were expensive college texts that he had managed to purchase secondhand during the summer.

"You can't take all that stuff to school!" I admonished John, with much less humor than my father had shown me twenty-five years before.

To my surprise, John agreed.

"You're right," he said. "I'll never be able to store all this stuff in my dorm room. I'll have to sacrifice something."

And he did. He gave up the textbooks.

Like dutiful parents, we accompanied John to the state university in Lincoln, Nebraska, where he had been assigned a room in Abel Hall. There is an excellent branch of Nebraska University in our own Omaha, but of course John was not about to go there; that would mean living at home for four more years! John wasn't too happy about our "tagging along" ("You didn't take me to kindergarten; why should you take me to college?"), but like all college alums, I was afflicted with "back-to-school fever" and was determined to spend at least a few hours reveling in the nostalgia which would surely be aroused by the familiar aura of a college dorm.

I was first aware of just how drastically things had changed when my husband and I followed John into the elevator of his dormitory. In my old dormitory elevator at Duchesne College, there had been a permanent odor of incense wafting from the nearby chapel, and on weekend evenings the incense mingled pleasantly with the faint fragrance of our perfume.

The "aura" of John's elevator bore the unmistakable "fragrance" of fast food, stale cigarettes, and unwashed sweat socks. But then one could hardly expect a men's dormitory to smell of girl's perfume!

As we stepped off the elevator on the thirteenth floor (we

thought it hilariously suitable that John's dorm was one of the few buildings in existence to claim a thirteenth floor), I said:

"Hold it. Wait a minute; something's not right here."

"What's the matter, Ma?" asked John as he juggled books, record albums, and a lamp.

"We're in the wrong building, that's what's the matter," I said, wondering why he couldn't see the obvious.

"No, we're not," he said. "This is Abel Hall; I've got my assignment right here in my pocket."

"But look!" I cried, pointing to the people scurrying up and down the corridors. "This is a girls' dormitory!"

"Oh, Ma," laughed John, "this is a coed dorm. The girls live on the even floors and the boys live on alternate floors."

"Then why are there girls on your alternate floor?" I asked.

"Because the top floor is for 'afterthoughts,' kids who registered late. Both boys and girls live on this floor."

"Do you mean to tell me," I exclaimed in disbelief, "that you are going to share living quarters with girls?"

"We don't share 'living quarters,' Mom," said John with impatience; "we just share the residence, just like I shared our house with Mary, Peggy, and Annie."

"Not like *that*, I hope," quipped his dad. "You'll get arrested for cruel and inhumane harassment."

"Don't panic, Mom," said John. "The girls are all at one end of the floor and the guys are at the other end."

"And the girls never come down to your end, right?" I asked hopefully.

"Only during visiting hours, Ma," said John, and I was tremendously relieved . . . until I found out that visiting hours were from 6 A.M. to 2:30 A.M.

I needn't have worried, for while rumor drifted home to us that John's dorm room was frequently visited by beautiful girls, it was seldom visited by John. Actually, it was not so much rumor, as it was proof positive provided by the telephone company. Whenever I would call John on his room phone (and I could call in the middle of the day or the middle of the night, it made no difference), he was never there, a fact I met with mixed emotions because somebody *was* there and that somebody was almost always of the opposite sex.

When John came home for Christmas I complained that I could never seem to catch him in his room, and he explained that he was spending little time in his dorm room as the dorm was too noisy for either studying or sleeping. (I dared not ask him where he had been sleeping, and I didn't need to ask him where he had been studying, as his report cards indicated he hadn't been too bothered with that particular aspect of college.)

We both concluded that he would be better off living in an apartment, so the next semester he and his former roommate moved into a small apartment in Lincoln.

The following fall, when John's brother Michael registered at the University of Nebraska at Lincoln, I was dismayed to learn that he had asked to be assigned a room in Abel Hall.

"Why do you want to live in a dorm?" I asked. "Why can't you live with John? I can't afford to 'furnish' another dorm room; I thought we would never get all John's stuff moved down to Lincoln."

"Calm down, Mom," said Mike. "Things are different today than they were in John's day." One would have thought he was referring to a generation gap rather than a two-semester time span.

"Different?" I asked suspiciously. "How different?"

"In the first place," said Mike, "I won't be hauling a bunch of miscellaneous stuff down to the dorm. Of course, I will need more luggage than John did. College kids today don't live in jeans and T-shirts anymore. I figure I will need a couple of three-piece suits, some sport coats, slacks, loafers, dress shoes, tennis shoes, and running shoes, half a dozen shirts, some ties, pajamas (pajamas? I didn't even know he *knew* about pajamas!), a robe, socks, underwear, and two tuxedos."

"*Two* tuxedos?" I asked incredulously. (Why do I ask?)

"Sure," he said. "You don't expect me to wear a winter tux to the spring dances, do you?"

Somehow I think I preferred the ridiculous remnants John called clothes. *Those* I could afford.

"At least we won't have to rent a moving van for your miscellaneous stuff," I said to Mike. "What *are* you taking? Should I save a couple of grocery cartons for you to pack things in?"

"Not necessary, Mom," said Mike cheerfully. "My 'miscellany' will fit right here in the old wallet."

"What do you mean?" I asked. (There I go, asking again!) "What kind of miscellany will fit in your billfold?"

"Your MasterCharge card!" said Mike confidently. "That will take care of everything I need. . . . Unless, of course, you'd rather give me cash?"

That noise you hear is my father in heaven, roaring with laughter.

21

Letters

Academic Dean
University of Nebraska
Lincoln, Nebraska

Dear Dean:

Thank you for your letter regarding our son, 486-30-1223, who is currently enrolled at the University of Nebraska.

I appreciate your concern that the lad has been in residence at the University for five semesters and has accumulated only 9 credit hours. We, too, are a trifle concerned about this; downright stunned, as a matter of fact, for we have canceled checks proving payment for a total of 65 credit hours.

Upon receipt of your letter, we called our son for an explanation.

After 13 unanswered calls to his dormitory room, seven unsuccessful "Hold on; I'll page hims" at the Student Center; four interesting if fruitless calls to Bill's Bar and Grill, and one call to a certain apartment on N Street, we contacted 1223, and he explained the situation as follows:

In his first semester he enrolled for 15 credit hours, but dropped Economics because it was an Upper Level Course. (It was also an 8 A.M. class, but I'm sure that is irrelevant.) As the semester drew to a close, he opted for three Incompletes on the theory that if he could spend Christmas vacation polishing up some term papers, he would get an A in each of those courses. He said: "Gee I thought I had turned those papers in." . . . He will look through his things and get back to me. (Don't hold your breath; I've seen "his things"; this could take months.)

In his second semester, he signed up for 12 hours, but dropped two Science courses and added two Business courses, which, unfortunately, he didn't get credit for because he was auditing one and taking one for credit, but he forgot which was which and took the wrong exam. He also got another Incomplete that semester, but it wasn't really his fault, as the professor rescheduled the final exam and failed to notify him. (I asked him if he had checked the Bulletin Board, and he went into a fit of hysterical laughter.)

In his third semester, he fell in love. (He claims "it's a silly rule, that one should have to attend class to get credit for the course.")

In his fourth semester, he signed up for 15 hours, dropped 6, added 3, and switched sections in English and Psychology but forgot to notify the Registrar, so he didn't get credit for either course. The Incomplete in Chemistry will be replaced with a grade just as soon as he pays for the lab equipment.

In his fifth semester, he switched his major, negating the 15 hours he had signed up for, but he claims the semester wasn't wasted because his dorm team won the Intramural Ping-Pong Tournament.

He assures us that this semester "everything is copacetic,"

though he is a little worried that he "may not get into Law School when the time comes."

I assured him that problem did not seem to be too pressing. Thank you for your concern.

Sincerely,

Dear MasterCharge:

In re: my January bill. I am puzzled by a charge of $473.22 for room, restaurant, and bar bills at the Hawaiian Village Hotel. As I have never been, am not presently, or have hopes of ever being in Honolulu, it is obvious that there is some mistake. Please remove the charges from my account.

Sincerely,

Dear MasterCharge:

In re: my February bill. I am somewhat perturbed to see that the January charge for $473.22 (plus finance charges) has not yet been removed from my account, and there is yet another charge which obviously cannot be mine. If I was going to go to Tokyo, I certainly wouldn't be spending $72 in a geisha house! In fact, if I could afford to go to Tokyo, I wouldn't; I'd go to Honolulu instead and whoop it up at the Hawaiian Village. As I have done neither, I would appreciate your removing both charges from my account.

Sincerely,

Dear MasterCharge:

This is getting ridiculous. $96 worth of Singapore Slings in "The Bar that Slung the First Sling?" Please cancel my account immediately, and while I have no intention of paying this bill, I would be interested in seeing the signed receipts. It isn't easy to misread a name like BLOOMINGDALE, but somebody in your office has obviously done exactly that.

Sincerely,

Dear MasterCharge:

Thank you for the receipts enclosed in my April bill. A check for the full amount is attached, with my apology. Due to the large amount, is it all right if I wait till next month to pay the $122 charged at the Pago Pago Playboy Club?

Humbly,

My dear son Jim:

How is everything in the Marine Corps? Your father says to tell you he is quite concerned about the "squalid living conditions" you have had to endure since your South Pacific assignment. What with all those "mosquito-infested swamps," "guerilla warfare in the jungle wilds," and "the long, boring hours on guard duty," your life must be simply awful . . . but not as awful as it's going to be if you don't send back my MasterCharge card *pronto*. I would also appreciate a money order covering the enclosed receipts.

And just out of curiosity, what did you buy in Tiffany's of Tasmania? A Mother's Day gift, perhaps?

Love,
Mother

Dear Mr. Prosecuting Attorney:

In re: your letter asking for the address of our son who is currently enrolled at the University of Nebraska in Lincoln, I have a few questions:

1. If I give you his last address, and it proves to be his current address, will you ask him why he doesn't answer my letters?

2. If I give you his address, do you really think you will ever catch him at home?

3. If I give you his address, and you find that he is still living there, am I responsible for his rent?

4. If I give you his address, and you go there and a tall, gorgeous blonde answers the door, I don't want to know about it.

5. Just what is the warrant for?

Sincerely,

Dear Mr. Prosecutor:

Overdrafts? You mean you *arrest* people for overdrawing on their accounts? Boy, am I glad I don't live in *your* county.

I checked our son's current address, and it seems it is a past address, but I will track him down for you. (You didn't happen to run into that blonde, did you? I'll wager *she* knows where he is.)

Sincerely,

Dear Mr. Prosecutor:

I contacted our son, who claims that he is absolutely unaware of the fact that he has been bouncing checks all over Lancaster County. A simple telephone call to his bank cleared up the whole matter.

It seems that our son, in preparing to go to college last fall, deposited his summer savings in an Omaha checking account. But on arriving in Lincoln, he found a bank which offered "free checking" to students, so he transferred his funds to the Lincoln bank.

He then inadvertently put the wrong checkbook into his wallet, and thus spent the next six months writing checks on the Omaha bank, while his funds rested in the Lincoln bank. When asked about overdraft notices, he admitted that as a matter-of-fact he had been getting a lot of letters from the Omaha bank, but he hadn't opened them; why should he, when he didn't have any money in their bank? Enclosed is my personal check to cover his overdrafts, fees, and fines. (I would appreciate it if you wouldn't cash this till the first of the month.)

Sincerely,

Dear Energy Commissioner:

In re: your recent suggestion that the country should go on a four-day work week in an attempt to save energy, I would like to offer a personal comment.

You're out of your mind.

Perhaps, in suggesting a four-day work week, you were not taking into consideration one particular group of workers: teachers. You do realize, I hope, that they, too, will want a four-day week (they are absolutely thrilled at your promise of a ten-hour day), which will mean that our children will be set free an extra day each week to consume energy.

Do you realize what this means? That every Friday (or Monday) when our children should be in schools, where they cannot control either the temperature or the lights, they will be at home washing their hair every ninety minutes (using up all the hot water with each shampoo), blasting away with hair dryers, heating up hot curlers or curling irons, and turning the home-heating thermostat to 82 degrees because they "are freezing with all that wet hair."

Their little brothers and sisters will be demanding that they be driven to the movies, the skating rink, the shopping center, the pizza parlor, or somebody's house, and if they are forced to stay home they, along with their older siblings, will be eating every hour on the hour, thus necessitating the use of the toaster, the oven, the can opener, the blender, the coffee maker, and the electric grill. I have not even mentioned the 1,746 times they will open the refrigerator and freezer doors, or the constant hassle over whose turn it is to use the washer and dryer.

It is obvious, therefore, that on this all-important "fifth day," the nation's energy consumption would increase, rather than decrease.

In point of fact, Mr. Commissioner, should you give our schoolchildren a three-day weekend, you will very likely deplete the nation's one most precious source of energy: mothers.

Sincerely,

Dear Mr. and Mrs. Zobernacki:

Thank you for the invitation to your daughter's wedding, about which there may be a little confusion.

On noting the name of the groom, we were somewhat surprised to see that it was very familiar; in fact, this was the first we had heard that our son was engaged to be married. The surprise was compounded by the fact that we have never heard him mention your daughter's name. On being shown the invitation, he said: "Is her name Maggie? That's funny, I always thought it was Maizie. Yeah, I think I remember her; nice kid, but she had this thing about getting married. So finally I said okay, get married! But I didn't mean to me! No way, man; I'm not gettin' married."

Please give Maggie (Maizie?) our congratulations. Not on getting married, but on getting out of it.

Sincerely,

22

Hold the Phone!

In 1975, when our home was destroyed by a tornado, I cried.

I didn't cry because our house was destroyed. That house was over one hundred years old and had long since lapsed into senility. (It wasn't "all there" upstairs.) The roof was literally rotting away, the ceilings were seriously considering falling down, and the bathrooms were in need of drastic repairs that could not be done because nobody made chain pulls anymore.

Furthermore, the entire house had become a haven for creatures from inner space. Waterbugs swam in our basement, mice camped out in our bedrooms, and our kitchen was a summertime picnic ground for every ant in the area.

We would have unloaded that house long before had it not meant attempting the impossible: cleaning the teenagers' bedrooms in anticipation of the inevitable Open House. When my mother heard that our teenagers' third-floor domain had

completely disappeared in the mouth of that monstrous tornado, she sighed: "I suppose there was really no other way. I
wonder how Teresa arranged it."

No, I did not cry because we lost our home. I cried because
we lost our telephones.

They were such nice telephones. Basic black, each had a
clear, loud ring, and a big easy-to-read, easy-to-spin dial. But
best of all, those telephones never went anyplace. With no
forty-foot cords or unpluggable jacks, the phones stayed put.
When the phone rang, I didn't have to follow a cord under
somebody's bed to answer it.

I knew that buying a new house would necessitate choosing new telephones, and every modern homemaker can tell
you how traumatic that can be. Before installing the telephones in a new home, one must consult a Time and Space
Expert on Telephone Traffic, and confer with an Interior
Decorator on color, style, and design. I was going to have
enough trouble finding a home and refurnishing it for my
family of twelve; I just wasn't up to tackling new telephones
as well.

As the realtors showed me through one house after another,
I vetoed each and every one. One afternoon, after a competent lady realtor had taken me on a tour of a very lovely house
that seemed particularly well-suited to our family, I once
again failed to show any enthusiasm.

"Don't tell me you don't like this house!" she said. "It's perfect for you!"

"I love this house," I told her, "but it's the same old story:
no telephones."

"Of course there aren't any telephones," she said in exasperation. "When a resident moves out, the phones are removed. That's the custom."

"I know that," I said. "And isn't it silly? Some hard-work-
ing homemaker spent hours and hours color-coordinating and

strategically placing the telephones in this house, and now I'm going to have to start all over again, because the ever-efficient telephone company left nary a mark on a wall or a telltale wire to give me a clue as to the color and placement of the telephones."

"Don't worry about that," said the realtor cheerfully. "The phone company has service people to advise you on such matters."

And sure enough, the day we moved into our new home a representative from the telephone company came to the house bearing books and brochures meant to inspire me, but all they did was confuse me. Did I want a conventional dial, push-button, or tiny touchtone? Trimline, Empress, or French Provincial? Should my phone be one that sits on a desk, hangs on a wall, or hides in a box?

Personally, I was sold on the Patio Pay Phone, complete with booth, but my husband vetoed it. He said it was just a gimmick; the kids wouldn't really have to pay. I told him so what? They would have to go outside!

I finally chose the Trimline Touchtone because it was "on special" that month. (Note: Always ask what they mean by "on special." In this case, it meant "costs more.") As for the color, I didn't have to make a decision because all the "on special" phones they had left were ivory. (Another note: If you have children, do not install light-colored telephones. They soon become multicolored: ball-point-pen blue, peanut-butter brown, raspberry-jelly red, perma-mustard yellow, or just-plain-dirt black.)

I must admit that the service person was very efficient in setting up a telephone-traffic pattern. He spent all morning following our kids around the house and finally concluded that all the phones should be installed in the bathrooms. I vetoed that, though I did agree with his conclusion that we should have more telephones than we originally planned. (I think he had also concluded that we should have had fewer children than originally planned, but he was too kind to say so.)

After consulting copious notes, he recommended a phone in the living room with an extension in the kitchen and another extension in the third-floor master bedroom. He also advised us to install a teenline, perhaps in the kitchen, with an extension in the second-floor hall and another in the basement rec room.

I agreed to everything except the living-room phone. I wanted it in the front hall. He asked why.

"You don't understand big families," I told him. "Everybody uses the back door—kids, adults, even company. Consequently the front hall is always empty, and always quiet. It's the perfect place for a private phone conversation."

The service person looked a little perplexed, but he agreed to install the telephone in the front hall.

I had never lived in a split-level modern home, and was unaware of the accessibility of the front door. With no steep steps leading to a spacious front porch (and no driveway leading to the back door), everybody began to use our front door: company, the kids, delivery men, meter men, me, my husband, even my mother, and she had never in her life used a family front door.

With all the traffic in and out of the front door, therefore, our front hall became a conference center, a cloak room, a book depository, a boot room, a pathway for kids who weren't supposed to track through the living room, and, thanks to the uncarpeted tile floor, a rainy-day roller-skating rink. Who could talk on the telephone there?

Nobody. So everybody used the kitchen phones, which meant that everytime I tried to cook a meal I had to climb over two teenage sons, each talking to a different girl on a different line.

After a month or so of tripping over long legs, I ordered the kitchen phones off limits for everybody but me. The next morning I tried to call out on one of those phones and found that it was busy; somebody was using our bedroom extension. It was one of the kids, so I reminded them all that they had their own line; they must not talk on the main line.

That night, as I was soaking in the tub, the phone in our bedroom rang, and rang, and rang. I knew my husband was in the basement, so I yelled at the kids:

"Why doesn't somebody answer that?"

They yelled back: "You told us we couldn't talk on your phone!"

Later I carefully explained to them that they could *answer* the main line; they just couldn't call out on it.

The next day I again tried to call out on the kitchen main line, and again the extension was busy. I checked the front hall; nobody talking on that phone; it was buried under books and boots. I went upstairs and found Peggy perched on my bed, cheerfully chatting away on my telephone.

"I thought I told you not to use that telephone," I scolded her.

"But you said to answer it if it rang; it rang, and when I answered it, it was for me," she said.

"Well tell your friends to call you on the teenline," I told her.

"Oh this isn't any friend," said Peg. "This is Annie. She's downstairs and wanted to ask me something, so she called me from downstairs. Isn't this neat?"

Our telephone traffic became more complex when our eldest son got a job which required making many phone calls. So he had his own telephone installed, in his bedroom. He assured us that he would have his own listing, and pay his own bill. There would be no problem.

But there was a problem: his own answering service . . . namely, me. While the phone was installed in his bedroom, our son was installed on the road; he was home only on weekends. Which meant that if his phone was going to be answered, it would have to be answered by somebody installed at home. Good old Mom who can't leave a ringing phone unanswered.

I wouldn't have minded so much had there not been another problem. Somehow his telephone number got cross-computerized with the number for American Family Insurance Company, and while I don't object to running halfway across the house and up a flight of stairs to help my son sell insurance, I wasn't all that happy about helping out the competition. Though I reported the problem daily, AFI clients kept calling, to their own dismay as well as mine.

When our son was transferred to South Dakota, we gratefully removed his private line, though unbeknownst to us, he notified the telephone company to reroute any local calls to our main-line number.

Which meant, of course, that the calls for the American Family Insurance Company now came through on our main line. It did save a lot of footwork on my part, but somehow I still begrudged being a free answering service for AFI. Finally, in desperation, we had our telephone number changed, but this succeeded only in frustrating our friends and relatives who had to call the old number in order to get the new one. Their frustration, however, was nothing compared to the anger of the AFI clients who would misdial and get our son's number, only to be rerouted to our old number, then rerouted to our new number, then told they had a wrong number!

Soon after ridding ourselves of our son's line, we simplified matters even more by getting rid of our teenline. It was a drastic decision, causing anarchy among our adolescents, but one we were forced to take by the teenagers themselves. They almost ran us into bankruptcy. It wasn't just the late-at-night long distance calls to their cousins, or even the calls-made-on-a-dare to John Denver or the Bee Gees. It was the dumb calls . . . like forty-seven in one month to a little town in New England. A check with the New England number indicated it was no one we knew or had ever heard of, and in fact, the New England party did not remember talking to anyone in Nebraska, though, come to think of it, they had received a lot of calls lately when no one was on the line.

A competent telephone executive (and father of eight) finally figured it out. It seems that when the area code for that New England county was punched, followed by the seven-digit number called, the touchtone telephone played the first ten bars of "The Entertainer." I doubt that even I could have resisted that one.

Without a teenline, our main line was overloaded, and friends complained that they could never get in, so we switched to the then-new Call Waiting Line (necessitating yet another new telephone number which finally forced the long-suffering clients of American Family Insurance Company to use the telephone book). On a Call Waiting Line, a "click" will signal you that there is a call waiting. Thus you can put the first call on "hold" while you answer the second call, though you can't talk to both at the same time.

Unless you are Annie.

When our friends complained that they still got a busy signal, we investigated and discovered that our teenage Annie, who has spent most of her life on the telephone, had no qualms at all about "holding" one boy on the first line, while chatting with another boy on the second.

"Something has to be done," I told my husband in frustration. "My friends don't mind getting a busy signal, but my editors are complaining. I can't conduct a career as a writer

and lecturer if editors and agents can't contact me. We will
just have to reinstall the teenline."

"We'll do better than that," he said. "We'll install a Mama
line; a private line, just for you alone. We'll get you an un-
listed number which you can give to your editors, agents, and
close friends. The kids won't be allowed to call out on that
line, and they won't be getting any calls on it because nobody
will know the number."

"That's a marvelous idea!" I told him, and it was. For the
next few weeks I had not only a private telephone for my professional calls, but a unique ring on the phone indicated that
this was a professional call and I must drop everything to answer it.

Which I did, last Tuesday. When my private phone rang,
I was positive it was my publisher calling, and in my hurry to
answer the phone I dropped a dozen eggs, breaking every one
of them. I left the mess and grabbed the phone.

It was not my publisher. It was Patrick.

"Patrick!" I said furiously. "What are you doing on this telephone?"

"Talking to you," he said truthfully.

"But how did you get this number?" I asked.

"By accident," he admitted cheerfully. "When I was in the
den the other day your phone rang and when I answered it a
voice said: 'Is this 556-8019? This is Radio Station KOIL
calling; do you know the secret word?' And I said: 'No, but
now I know the secret number!'"

"But, Patrick," I said, "why didn't you call on the other
line? Why did you call on this number?"

"'Cause I knew you'd answer it quick," he explained, "and
I only got a minute before the principal comes back to his
office. Do you know what today is, Mom?"

"It's Tuesday, Patrick," I said with a sigh. One never
knows what Pat has on his mind.

"It's also your birthday, Mama. Happy Birthday! I love you! I gotta go now. Bye!"

Well, after all, it *is* a professional line, and I *am* a professional mother!

23

L'Affaire de Mimi

Everybody at our house is in a funky mood because of Mimi.

Until recently, Mimi was the most cheerful member of our family. Always happy, bouncy, and vivacious, she would never allow any of the rest of us to be despondent. If any of us would be sick, or sad, or just have a bad day, Mimi could be counted on to cheer us up with lots of love and crazy antics to make us laugh.

But it has been awful around here lately because Mimi herself has become despondent. She got jilted.

When that handsome jerk moved in across the street, I knew we were in for trouble, because the first time he made a neighborly call, he had eyes for no one but Mimi, and she was obviously smitten. I tried to warn Mimi that this guy

looked like a flighty fellow to me, but Mimi had lost her heart
to him, and there was nothing we could do about it. Within
weeks, the two of them were carrying on a scandalous affair,
and as I anticipated, it was as brief as it was passionate. As
soon as the cad "had his way" with our darling Mimi, he
jilted her, leaving her with a broken heart and you can guess
what else.

It is really not so shocking or sad when one realizes that
Mimi is not a person, but a poodle . . . though many poodle
owners will claim poodles are people. Poodles are so bright, so
quick, so affectionate, and so loyal, they tend to become a part
of the family, causing just as much concern, joy, and heart-
ache as the human members do.

While Mimi's affair was not particularly shocking, it was a
surprise, for in all the years we have had her, Mimi has never
once stooped to indulging in sex for the single poodle.

When we adopted Mimi, she was only six weeks old, and
(supposedly) a pure-bred poodle, and I must admit that I
had visions of breeding her and growing rich off the profits
produced by her progeny. Toy poodles were the rage; everyone wanted one, and as a consequence, a poodle pup would
bring a nice fee, while an entire litter could pay a year's tuition for a non-poodle collegiate.

However, as soon as Mimi became old enough to "incorpo-
rate" she refused to cooperate. We introduced her to one pros-
pect after another, but Mimi would have none of them. She
would brush off a lover's advances with a ladylike growl,
throw her nose in the air, and glance at me as if to say that,
unlike *some* people in this family, she had no intention of
contributing to the population explosion.

Mimi preferred the celibate life, but while she may have
been pure in thought, she was not so pure in background.
Someplace along the line a dachshund had obviously slipped
into her family tree or, more likely, her family dog house, and

Mimi, acquiring the characteristics of her dachshund grand-daddy, grew too long to be good-looking. Let's face it: she was downright ugly.

Perhaps it was her lack of good looks that made her seek the life of a recluse, but I doubt it. It seemed more likely that her Aryan bloodline supplied a superiority complex which caused her to feel that all males were chauvinists, unworthy of her favors.

At least, that was the way Mimi acted until Chi-Chi came along.

Chi-Chi was a tiny chihuahua who moved into the house across the street and, under the guise of a neighborly visit, seduced our celibate spinster. To the chagrin of our neighbors, and to the delight of our kids, what began as a playful canine caper soon progressed to puppy love, and eventually to a full-blown affair. Mimi and Chi-Chi had no shame. They "carried on" in the front yard, in the back yard, in the middle of the driveway, in the middle of the day . . . and in the middle of the night.

For Chi-Chi, like so many modern adolescent males, had no respect for time and frequently called on Mimi in the wee hours of the morning. When Chi-Chi would bound onto our porch and begin his love howl, Mimi would bound into our bedroom and announce with excited and anticipatory barking that she was ready and willing and would somebody please let her out!

Night after night my husband would threaten: "If you let that dumb dog out, I will kill both of you." And I would respond: "Don't be silly; Mimi is too old to get pregnant."

To which he, in turn, would shout: "Ha! I've heard *that* line before. Lock her up!"

But I was born with romance in my heart and felt that Mimi should be allowed one mad fling before middle age set in. So, under the pretense of taking her to the basement, I would slip downstairs and let Mimi out to meet her lover. Actually, I felt that a midnight rendezvous was preferable to those daytime assignations, the first of which caused Patrick to ask: "Mama, what's that doggie doing to Mimi?" and subsequent meetings which brought shouts of: "Hey, Mom, come watch; they're at it again!"

As one might have expected from such a passionate affair, the inevitable happened. The chauvinist Chi-Chi feasted and fled, leaving Mimi alone to face the music or, in this case, the veterinarian. For Mimi was not so old as I had thought, and it soon became apparent that she would become a parent.

That, however, was not a big problem. The big problem, as is often the case in such affairs, was "How to break the news to her father?" (Not her poodle father; her people father. Poodles are part people, remember?)

I reminded myself that, in the past, my husband had always been happily resigned when I would announce (annually) that we would soon be hearing the patter of little feet, but those were always the two-footed variety who provided, at the very least, an exemption on our income tax. I worried and fretted about how I should tell him of Mimi's nontaxable Coming Event, but as it turned out, I never had to tell him, for the Event came sooner than I anticipated.

How was I to know how long it takes to make a puppy? I had just assumed that puppy pregnancies were the same length as people pregnancies, so no one was more surprised than I when, less than three months after her assignation, Mimi went into labor.

That's not quite true; there was one more surprised than I. My husband. Due to Mimi's low-slung form and shaggy coat, her "condition" had never been obvious. Consequently, my husband did not know of the impending additions to our family until one morning when he went to his closet to get a clean shirt and shouted:

"Teresa! What in the hell is Mimi doing in my closet? TERESA WHAT THE HELL IS MIMI DOING?!!"

What Mimi was doing was producing four beautiful puppies. While my husband stomped around the bedroom fussing and fuming in angry frustration, our children came bounding into the room to witness that most miraculous of all events: an animal creature giving birth. For our city-dwelling kids this was a spectacular experience, and even my husband eventually became entranced, as our lively, never-still, always-adolescent Mimi became a grown-up mother . . . gentle, patient, suffering in silence, caring for each of her infants, cleansing them, kissing them, and protecting them from us people.

By midafternoon we were finally able to woo the new mama from the closet and lift her children gently into a blanket-lined box, which was to be their home for the next few weeks.

They were fun weeks. As the puppies slowly "came alive," opening their little eyes, giving huge yawns, they did little but eat and sleep. But eventually they learned to climb out of their box, to play with each other and with the children, and we took them to our hearts and to our carpeting.

"These pups have got to go," announced my husband each time they did exactly that, though I don't know why he complained so much; he never cleaned it up. But as soon as the pups were weaned, even I agreed that we must find homes for them. While I felt capable of caring for a big house, ten children, two dogs, and one husband, I was not about to add on the care and feeding of four choodles. (What else would you call a chihuahua-poodle?) We would have to get rid of the pups.

I soon learned a little-known fact of life: it is easier to get rid of a spouse than a puppy . . . and for a while I was afraid I might have to choose the easier route. While it may be true that toy poodles are in demand, it is also true that their part-poodle offspring are in deluge; there are a million of them available for the asking, which nobody ever does.

After much pleading and placating, we persuaded the cleaning lady to take a puppy (in exchange for windows and woodwork) and another pup became a gift to my godchild. (His mother threatened to revoke the christening, but she'll come around, just as soon as their cat has kittens.) A third puppy, the runt of the litter, decided that dog earth was for the birds (or, in our household, more likely "for the kids") and returned to dog heaven. That left us with the biggest and ugliest of the lot. If you think it's hard to get rid of a cute little puppy, just try to get rid of an ugly one.

We tried to foist him off on the monks at Mount Michael Abbey, but Father Abbot can say "no thanks" quicker than anyone I know, except for my mother, who didn't even wait to be asked.

Would the good nuns like a convent companion?

"What convent?" they asked cheerfully. "Our apartment doesn't allow pets."

The pastor claimed he would be happy to take a pup, but his curates would complain. (What are curates for, if not to take the blame?)

But the pastor did have a suggestion, and a solution. The church social was Sunday; perhaps we could raffle the puppy, and make a little money for the missions. So we did, and our ugly pup became a prize pup and went home with a happy little girl who held the winning ticket.

But an unhappy little boy hollered all the way home. Patrick will never forgive me for giving away his "best friend," and his brothers and sisters would have preferred that I give away Patrick. Even my husband claims he misses that little bark and tiny wagging tail, and he halfheartedly suggested that perhaps we could persuade Mimi to breed another brood.

A handsome male miniature poodle had just moved into the neighborhood, and I once again foresaw a fortune made from breeding pure poodles. So I agreed to set up a rendez-vous.

The miniature was most agreeable, but Mimi was not. She had renewed her vow of celibacy and would have none of this sex nonsense. Perhaps she is still carrying a torch for her Latin lover, but I think it is more likely that she figures four kids is quite enough, thank you, and she is not about to start another family.

In any event, she is no longer the same old Mimi. Her bounce is gone; her cheerful "yipe" has been replaced by a brusque bark, and she has made it quite clear that she would rather pout than play. I can't understand it.

"I know what's the matter with Mimi, Mama," said Tim one morning, when Mimi indicated that she was not a bit interested in playing her usual position of shortstop on their baseball team.

"What do you think it is, Tim?" I asked. "Old age?"

"Naw," said my son. "Mimi's just sad 'cause all her children have gone away. Won't you be unhappy when we're all grown up and gone?"

I plead the fifth.

24

The Marine
Him

"From the halls of Montezuma to the shores of Tripoli!" sing the Marines in their famous battle hymn.

Big deal. Anybody can make it from the halls of Montezuma to the shores of Tripoli. That's nothing to brag about. The biggest battle any Marine ever fought and won was not on foreign soil. It was a domestic war, waged in his mother's kitchen the day he announced:

"I am going to enlist in the Marines."

The first time our son Jim intimated that he wanted to join the United States Marine Corps, we were not too concerned. Despite the fact that he was determined to drop out of school and enlist, we were sure that even the most enthusiastic recruiter would hesitate to sign up a five-year-old who still had six months to go in kindergarten.

Jim's devotion to the Corps continued throughout grade school; he plastered his bedroom walls with Marine posters, spent his Saturday afternoons hanging out at the recruiting office, and pestered the Pentagon with letters demanding more and more information on the Marine Corps.

In high school, Jim's interest in the Marines was temporarily displaced by his fascination for a much more intimidating group: girls. Saturdays which had formerly been spent hanging around the recruiting office were now spent hanging around some girl's house. Plans for the future were forgotten in his enjoyment of the present.

But shortly after his eighteenth birthday, Jim came sailing out to the kitchen and exclaimed brightly:

"Hey, Mom! Guess what I did today?"

"Went to class, I hope!" I said angrily. "Your counselor called just a few minutes ago and said you missed chemistry class this morning. Where were you, anyway?"

"That's what I wanted to talk to you about, Mom," said Jim. "I'm just wasting my time in that chem class. I don't like it, I'll never use it, and, frankly, I don't think I can pass the course."

"Well you'd better pass it because you need the hours to graduate."

At the word "graduate," silence exploded in my kitchen.

"You *are* going to graduate, aren't you? I mean, nothing has come up to delay that diploma, has it?"

"Of course I'm going to graduate, Mom," said Jim. "I'm just not going to graduate from Westside. That's what I started to tell you . . . about what I did today. . . ."

And then I knew. He hadn't mentioned it for months, but I knew. The gradual reappearance of Marine posters, the accumulation of military mail . . . the frequent phone calls from men too deep voiced to be high school peers. The recruiters had finally begun to return those phone calls from the "little kid" who wanted to drop out of kindergarten and join the Marines.

"Mom, I enlisted in the Marines this morning," said Jim, and then his enthusiasm and excitement could be contained no longer.

"I'm a Marine!" he cried happily. "I take my physical next Saturday and leave for San Diego on the twenty-fifth. Don't be mad at me, Mom! Please don't be mad, when I'm so happy!"

Whereupon I burst into tears and spent the next six days sobbing hysterically, while my husband tried to placate me by making useless phone calls to the recruiter, the captain, and even the commandant, all of whom assured him that there was nothing we could do about it; the papers had been signed; Jim was committed to the Corps.

The fact that Jim was still legally a minor was evidently irrelevant.

"I don't believe this," I told the colonel in one of my calls. "Last week I had to sign a permission slip for Jim to go to the state football tournament. The week before I had to sign a permission slip for him to use the school trampoline. Are you going to tell me that a kid who can't go on the senior-class picnic without his parents' permission can, without their consent or even their knowledge, sign up for four years in the armed forces?"

"Unbelievable, but true," admitted the colonel.

"But Jim hasn't finished high school yet!" I wept.

"He will," said the colonel. "I promise you that Jim will get his diploma shortly after he finishes boot camp."

Despite Jim's assurance that he would not settle for a General Equivalency Diploma, but would insist on a diploma from a fully accredited high school (actually, he eventually

received his diploma from an exclusive Catholic prep school),
I was inconsolable. My only concept of the Marines had come
from the movies . . . thousands of boys being shot and killed
on a beach somewhere, or maybe never making it to the beach
because they had previously succumbed to the pressures and
persecutions inflicted on them in boot camp. I knew about
those Marines! I recalled with a shudder that terrible movie
where Jack Webb, as the sadistic drill instructor, mentally
and physically abused the Marine recruits until they literally
fell dead at his feet. (Of course I saw a lot of John Wayne's
Marine movies, too, but hard as I would try to conjure up
memories of that kind gentleman, John Wayne, mean old
Jack Webb kept snarling his way back into my con-
sciousness.)

I began to feel a little better about the Marines when Jim
received his first set of Orders. After stating his date of departure and destination, the Orders concluded with a sentence which would warm the heart of any mother who has
ever packed a kid off to camp or college:

"The recruit will proceed to his destination with no personal property other than the clothes he is wearing, and carrying no cash in excess of five dollars."

You can't beat a deal like that!

But my positive attitude was somewhat dampened by the
first letter we received from boot camp. The letter was not
from Jim, but rather from his commanding officer, whose
name I can't recall for the simple reason that I never knew it.
While the letter itself was typed, the signature was written in
longhand, an illegible squiggle impossible to decipher . . . a
fact which surely caused more than one Marine mother to
wonder if the CO felt that, under the circumstances, it was
propitious for him to remain anonymous, or if the fellow had
just never learned how to write his name.

The letter welcomed us to the Marine family, and then

launched into an explanation, meant, I suppose, to allay our fears about boot camp. It warned that while we would soon be getting a letter from our son, we should not take too seriously anything he might say, as recruits tend to overreact to boot camp, exaggerating the behavior of the drill instructors, imagining injustices and ill-treatment, and taking out of context comments and criticisms that are made for their own good. We were assured that the methods employed by the Marines would "make a man of your son" and "may save his life someday."

I read the letter, and if that colonel thinks Marine recruits tend to overreact, he should meet up with more Marine mothers. Before I had reached the illegible signature, I had the telephone in my hand, determined to call my congressman, the Secretary of Defense, the President of the United States, and maybe even Jack Webb.

"Wait a minute," said my husband. "Here's another letter at the bottom of the pile, and this one's from Jim! Let's see what he has to say."

The colonel was right. Jim was definitely overreacting to boot camp, though not quite in the manner his CO had anticipated.

"This place is terrific!" Jim wrote on his third day in boot camp. "We work our tails off, but I have never felt so good, and I am sure that I have chosen a great career. Of course, it's not all roses around here; the drill instructors yell at us all the time (really makes me feel at home!), but one sergeant told me he thought I had the makings of a real Marine." (I hope that wasn't one of the "comments taken out of context.")

There was only one sentence in the letter which indicated that perhaps Jim might be exhausted to the point of hallucinating.

"I don't even mind getting up so early in the morning," he wrote, "because the breakfasts here are so good!" I assumed that letter had not been censored by the Marines, or surely Jim would have been discharged as a Section 8.

In the three years that Jim has been in the Corps, his father and I have come to appreciate all that the Marines have taught him, talents that will never be attributed to his college-age siblings: how to make a bed, how to hang up his clothes, how to peel potatoes, how to write a letter home.

However, there are a few points they failed to pick up on, and I offer them here to the Joint Chiefs of Staff, or whomever, with the suggestions that they be incorporated into every military manual.

1. Servicemen who telephone their parents long distance should note that there are little slots at the top of the telephone which have been put there for their convenience. When coins are deposited in these slots, it becomes unnecessary for the serviceman placing the call to tell the operator: "Reverse the charges, please."

2. Servicemen who are stationed outside the continental United States should be periodically briefed on such subjects as Time Zones, and a regulation instituted whereby any serviceman placing a call should first consult his watch and remind himself that while it may be only 9 P.M. *his* time it is 2 A.M. *Mom's* time, and if her phone rings in the middle of the night, she may not live long enough to answer it. Servicemen placing such untimely calls should also be aware of the fact that telephone calls at two in the morning do not make Dads too receptive to requests for money . . . (and why else are you calling, kid?).

3. When home on leave, servicemen should remember that little brothers and sisters "aren't slaves, and just 'cause you're a Marine you can't boss us around!" (Also, servicemen should be made aware of the fact that their little brothers and sisters

have memorized the paragraph in the Uniform Code of Military Justice which prohibits a serviceman from harassing or hitting any civilian, including, and maybe even especially, a sibling civilian.)

4. When home on leave, servicemen are advised to wear dress uniform on the following "official" occasions: the day your mother entertains her bridge foursome, the night your dad drags you to the club stag, the evening your sister asks you to pick her up at her sorority meeting, and the afternoon your little brother hosts his cub scout den. While it is only *recommended* that you wear dress uniform on the above-mentioned occasions, it is *mandatory* that you appear in full-dress uniform when you go to visit your grandmother.

5. In writing letters home, servicemen are advised to make frequent references to such topics as: college courses you are allegedly studying in your free time, historical places or far-flung relatives you promised your parents you would visit, and (a sure winner) the subject of last Sunday's sermon at church. Topics to be avoided include: the perilous parachute jump you must make tomorrow morning, the explosive devices you are learning how to detonate, the beer-drinking record you broke in Hong Kong, and the island lovelies who "hang around the barracks begging to do laundry and other things for the guys."

I didn't want to be a Marine mother, but after many months of reading Jim's letters, meeting his peers and their families, and learning just what the United States Marine Corps is and does, I must admit that I am proud to bear the title of "Marine Mom." I think my love affair with the Corps began the day Jim graduated from boot camp. His father and I attended the graduation ceremonies at the Marine Corps Recruit Depot in San Diego, and I don't know when I have been so moved by "pomp and circumstance."

It was a beautiful June morning, Southern California at its best. After a tour of the base, parents of the graduates gathered in the auditorium where we were shown a film explaining the rigorous training our sons had just completed.

When the lights came up, we were introduced to the drill instructors, the platoon leaders, and the company commander, who bragged unabashedly about his men who only a short time ago had been our boys.

After the conferring of diplomas and the recognition of honor graduates, the new Marines marched to the parade grounds where the Colors were presented, and the Marine hymn and the National Anthem were played by the Marine band.

At the final command: "Company dismissed!" the stiff-backed, straight-faced Marines suddenly became kids again, jumping for joy, grabbing each other by the shoulders, then running to find and hug their parents and girlfriends.

And I, who had shed so many tears of sorrow at the thought of my son enlisting in the Marines, shed a few more tears . . . of pride . . . that my son was now one of "The Few. The Proud. The Marines."

However . . . lest you think I have been completely indoctrinated, I do have one tiny criticism of the Corps.

If you Marines are going to continue showing that film on boot camp to Marine parents, don't you think it would be a good idea to find a narrator other than Jack Webb?

25

Sleeping Over

"Peggy is certainly getting to be polite," mumbled my husband when he came back to bed after a middle-of-the-night raid on the refrigerator.

"Why do you say that?" I asked sleepily.

"Because I just stuck my head in her room to say good night, and she said: "Good night, Mr. Bloomingdale.""

"That wasn't Peggy," I said. "That's Sandy Haller; she's sleeping over with Annie tonight."

"Sleeping over?" he asked. "I assume that means she's spending the night here; where did you get the term 'sleeping over'?"

"From the kids," I sighed, wondering why a man who will sit in absolute silence, with his nose in a book, from suppertime till bedtime, can find so much to talk about at 3 A.M. "That's what the kids call staying all night with a friend; it's a phrase of their generation."

Only the terminology is of their generation; the custom of "sleeping over" goes back as far as I can remember. I wouldn't be surprised if the caveman's kids begged permission to stay all night in somebody else's cave. (I hasten to add that despite what my children would have you believe, I was never personally acquainted with any cavemen.) Spending the night with her best friend is a highlight of any little girl's life, for there is the fun of staying up late, and having special treats, and lying awake in the midnight darkness telling ghost stories, and trading secrets one would never dare share with a sister.

"Sleeping over" is not to be confused with slumber parties. The former is a one-guest overnighter, the latter a multiguest all-nighter, which can be distinguished by the fact that the father of the hostess inevitably ends up taking a sleeping pill while the mother of the hostess resorts to No-doze tablets.

Slumber parties were more indigenous to my day, when homes were bigger and parents more patient. When one or the other of my four sisters or I would give a slumber party in my parents' huge house, my father did not settle for a sleeping pill; instead he checked into a hotel for the night. (No one ever gossiped about my father's occasional overnight stay at the Robidoux Hotel, for he always explained the situation the next day in his newspaper column "Timely Observations," where he would recant the joys of listening to a houseful of teenage girls. Such columns would always delight our guests, as they loved to have their names mentioned, but we, being typical teenage daughters, were embarrassed by the notoriety. My mother, on the other hand, would read those columns on our slumber parties and comment with a loving sigh: "I wish I knew as little about it as he does.")

On the nights of our slumber parties, my mother never had to take a No-doze, for my mother was *always* awake. To my knowledge, my mother did not go to bed throughout my entire youth. I can remember, in my teens, coming in from late dates always to find Mother still up. (Waiting, I suspected years later, for a call to come downtown and identify the body.) And no matter how early I got up in the morning, Mother would already be down in the kitchen, cooking breakfast.

This would be especially true on the morning after a slumber party, where my friends and I would stumble down to the kitchen to find Mother ready to serve bacon and eggs, homemade coffee cake, and hot chocolate. No wonder my slumber parties were so popular!

Today's teenagers are too sophisticated for slumber parties (or perhaps the homes are too small, or the mothers too busy), but kids still love to "sleep over."

Frankly, I always dread it when one of my kids asks to have a friend sleep over. With our big family, it means not only a reshuffling of bed assignments (Peggy's guest will sleep in Annie's bed; Annie will sleep in Dan's bed; Dan will move in with Patrick, which means that Tim will have to sleep on the couch) but also a short course in Language. ("You boys watch your language when there are guests in the house!") Then, of course, there is the compulsory housecleaning, for I am always sure that a guest will notice the cobwebs in the corner of the basement or the mold on the bacon in the back of the refrigerator.

But even more, I dread it when one of my kids asks permission to "sleep over" at somebody else's house. I wouldn't mind it so much if Somebody Else also had a big family and my child would most likely be bunking in a sleeping bag and sharing a bathroom with eight other kids. But such never seems to be the case. My children always seem to pal around with kids who are either rich or planned. (The children in the household never outnumber the bedrooms.)

I remember the first time our eldest daughter slept over at a friend's house, Mary was then about seven or eight years old, and on reluctantly returning to her humble abode, she exclaimed: "Oh, Mom, you should see Carol's house! It's gorgeous! Her mother asked me if I wanted to sleep in their guest bedroom, but I said I'd rather sleep in the other bed in Carol's room. Can you imagine having your own bedroom with two beds in it!"

"There are three beds in your bedroom," I reminded her.

"Yes," replied Mary scornfully, "and they are full of sisters! When can I get my own room?"

"As soon as six of your siblings move out," I told her. "Now go wash your hands for dinner."

"I can't," she said. "Jim's in the bathroom, and Mike's waiting to get in, and John's telling them both to hurry up. I may never get into the bathroom again! Carol has her own bathroom!"

"Good for Carol," I said sarcastically, then tried another tack. "I bet Carol would trade anything for a little sister."

"Do you really think she would?" asked Mary.

"I'm sure of it," I said.

"Good!" said Mary. "I'll call her right now and offer to trade our Peggy for Carol's canopy bed."

Another problem with "sleep overs" is the one-upmanship among Mothers. Mothers who ordinarily wouldn't let their kids eat so much as a graham cracker before bedtime suddenly turn into pastry chefs when somebody sleeps over. When our Peg stays all night with her friend Amy, Amy's mother (who hasn't chipped a chocolate in years) produces a big batch of Tollhouse cookies for the girls to nibble on while they watch TV.

Which means, of course, that when Amy comes to our house, I must produce something equal or better in the way of gourmet treats, as well as fix the long-broken aerial on the TV set.

When our kids got a little older, I was not so concerned about what they were eating when they slept over at somebody else's house, as what they were *doing*. Were they still content to watch TV, tell stories, or trade secrets? Or were they up to more sophisticated things, like smoking in the bathroom, or tasting samples from the host's liquor cabinet? Or were they even there at all?

I got a call one Friday night about eleven-thirty from a pharmacist friend of ours who was just closing his store.

"I thought I'd better call you," he said with some concern. "Your daughter was in here with a friend just a minute ago; I figured they had been to the football game and had come in to use the phone to call home for a ride, but she said, No, thanks; they'd walk home. I know how you feel about your kids walking home this late at night. . . ."

"Thanks for calling," I said, and hurriedly hung up the phone, then immediately called the mother of the friend with whom our daughter was "sleeping over."

"She's not here, Teresa," said the mother when I asked about my daughter. "My Beth's been sick all week; she hasn't had any friends over."

After a frantic hour of telephoning, we found our daughter comfortably housed with another Beth . . . the one who lives next door to the pharmacy. (Note: Always get the name, age, and serial number of the person with whom your kid is "sleeping over.")

On another occasion, our daughter Peg had asked permission to invite her friend Lynnette to spend the night.

"We have to be up at school at seven-thirty Saturday morning for a meeting," said Peg, "and Lynnette's folks are out of town, so she's staying with her sister who won't be able to drive her to school and it's too far to walk; so can Lynnette sleep over Friday night?"

"I guess so," I said, still trying to interpret Peg's explana-

tion, "but if you girls are going to the football game, remind
Lynnette that your curfew is midnight."

"Oh, we'll be home before that," said Peg, "'cause we've
got to get up early in the morning."

And, in fact, Peg came in at ten-thirty, but she was alone.
"Where's Lynnette?" I asked.

"We sort of got separated," said Peg. "There was a whole
bunch of us, in two cars, and I got in Ann's car, but Lynnette
went with Martha. Don't worry about her; she should be here
any minute."

The minute stretched into an hour. No Lynnette.

"Stop worrying, Mother," said Peg. "Lynnette knows she
has to be in by midnight. It's only eleven-thirty."

The midnight curfew came and went without Lynnette. At
twelve-thirty we called Martha, only to discover that her
phone was out of order. I lay awake all night worrying about
Lynnette and wondering how I would explain to her parents
that their darling daughter had disappeared.

Peg went off to school at seven-thirty, and a few minutes
later she called to tell me that Lynnette was there, safe and
sound.

"What happened to her?" I asked wearily.

"She said Martha had a flat tire, and it took so long to get
it changed it was almost one o'clock by the time they got
home."

"But why didn't Lynnette come here?" I asked.

"It was so late, she didn't want to wake everybody up, so
she just stayed all night at Martha's. See, Mother, I told you
not to worry!"

Oh, yeah? And just what does she think kept Lynnette so
safe and sound? My worrying, that's what!

I am always worried when my children's friends "sleep
over" at our house, even when they actually show up to sleep.
I worry that the bed may not be comfortable enough, or the

towels clean enough, or the little kids quiet enough, and I always have visions of our guest returning home the next morning to tell her parents: "If you think my bedroom's a mess, you should see some of those Bloomingdale bedrooms!" (Our Dan cannot understand why he must clean up his room when his sister has a friend over.)

The only time I am really comfortable with overnight guests are the rare occasions when my nieces or nephews come to visit their cousins. Last summer, Annie and Peg played hostess to four of their cousins: my sister Madeleine's younger daughters, Mini and Kathleen Sanders; my sister Janet's only daughter, Suzanne Schiesl; and my sister Betsy's youngest daughter, Brigid Morrison. Because the girls' bedroom could not accommodate six girls, they all slept on quilts and comforters on the family-room floor. All close in age (and looking so much alike they could have been sextuplets), the girls had a marvelous time giggling and chatting and telling each other fantastic tales of their riotous brothers. They got a little carried away, however, and about 3 A.M. I had to shush them up. Only it was a bit more than a shush; for a mother to be heard over six gabbing girls, she must shush with a shout.

"Okay, girls!" I shouted over the din of the stereo and conversation. "That's it! To bed! Each and every one of you sack out right this minute; shut the mouth as well as the eyes. Have you got that?"

For a moment there was dead silence, then the daughters of my three sisters burst out laughing and said, almost simultaneously: "You sound just like my mother!" For a moment I was whirled back in time, to my own teenage slumber parties, and suddenly I realized I sounded just like *my* mother!

I suppose children reach an age when they no longer like to "sleep over" at their friends' homes. At least I hope that's so. The other night we were discussing that very topic when one of my children said:

"Speaking of 'sleeping over,' Mom, is it okay if I sleep over at Candy's Friday night?"

I told him to cut out the clowning and get back to studying for his college comps.

I guess a mother must always concern herself about the "where" and "with whom" her children are spending the night. And, believe me, you can't be too careful; you must get all the details of the child's plans. I found that out not long ago when our daughter Annie asked permission to spend an entire weekend with her friend, Sandy Haller. Now I like Sandy; she's a grand girl, comes from a wonderful family, so I told Annie okay.

"You may go skating or to a movie," I told Annie as she was packing her overnight bag. "Maybe I'd better give you some money. How much do you think you will need?"

"Oh, I'd say about four hundred dollars," said Annie.

"Four hundred dollars!" I said. "What on earth would you need all that money for?"

"The plane fare," said Annie. "Have you forgotten? Sandy moved to California!"

26

TV or Not TV?

"How come you hate television?" my son griped last Saturday when I switched off the boob tube and suggested he do something a bit more intellectual, like take out the garbage.

"I don't hate television," I said, "as long as the show is something worthwhile. I just don't consider that test pattern you were watching worthwhile."

"That wasn't a test pattern, Mom," he said. "That was a close-up of this week's winner on the Amateur Art Show."

"You were watching an art show?" I asked incredulously.

"Not exactly," he admitted. "I was waiting for "Gilligan's Island" to come on."

"Good Lord!" I said. "Even Gilligan has stopped watching "Gilligan's Island." You have seen so many of those reruns you must know every script by heart. Why won't you read a good book? TV is such a waste of time!"

"Mom, how can you be so critical of TV when you never watch it?" he asked.

"I watch enough TV to know you watch too much TV!" I told him. "What makes you think I never watch it?"

"Because," he said, "last summer when the whole country was asking 'Who shot J.R.?' you were asking 'Who's J.R.?'"

"The fact that I do not watch 'Dallas' may make me un-American," I said, "but it does not mean I am uninformed. I am very much aware of the latest television shows . . . unfortunately."

"Oh, yeah?" he asked. "Then how come in last week's television poll you said that your favorite sit-com was 'The Donna Reed Show.'"

"Because that is my favorite show," I told him truthfully.

"But Donna Reed hasn't been on television in years!" he said.

"That's why she's my favorite," I replied. "Donna had the good sense to quit while she was ahead."

I admit that I am not too fond of TV, but that may be due to the fact that I was raised on radio. I grew up in an era when Jack Armstrong ruled the world, and "I Love a Mystery" made our day. As my kids are addicted to "M.A.S.H.," "Mork and Mindy," "Buck Rogers," and "Happy Days," I was addicted to "First Nighter," "Lux Radio Theater," "One Man's Family," and "Suspense." But my mother was not as frustrated by my radio addiction as I am with my own kids' TV addiction for the simple reason that radio had one great quality which television will never acquire: you didn't have to watch it. We could listen to the radio and become completely engrossed in the show, while at the same time we could clean our rooms, wash the dishes, or scrub and wax the kitchen floor. Our kids don't have time to do their chores, because they are too tied to the TV.

Or perhaps my prejudice toward television goes all the way

back to the beginning, though I do hate to admit that I am old enough to remember the beginning of television. Actually, I missed the beginning. When television was perfected to the point where it became a popular household item, I was not living in a household; for most of the year I was a boarder in a convent college dorm, where the nuns had just adjusted to radios and record players. Television would have been unthinkable.

Thus, it was not until I graduated and moved into an apartment with two other girls, one of whom was the owner of a secondhand console, that I got my first taste of TV and that first taste was bitter. Oh, the shows were very good (better than today's, in fact), but that was the problem. They were too good, and our Saturday-night dates refused to take us out until after the Sid Caesar "Show of Shows," which ended too late for us to catch the main feature at the Paramount or the best part of Peony Ballroom's Big Band dances.

In spite of Sid Caesar and Imogene Coca, I somehow managed to get married, but unlike today's newlyweds, my husband and I did not include a TV set among our first furniture priorities. In fact, we were married for three blissful years before we got our first set, and we wouldn't have gotten one then if it had not been for my mother-in-law. After we had made her a grandmother three times in three years, she bought us a television set and subtly suggested that we start watching the late show.

Thus began my lifelong antagonism toward television. Oh, it's not what you are thinking: TV did not jeopardize my marriage (in fact, we had seven more children in the next nine years). My husband couldn't care less about television. In truth, I can never remember him sitting through an entire Super Bowl game, and he once earned the scorn of his own children when he fell asleep during the final minutes of a tied football game between Nebraska and Oklahoma.

No, it was not Howard Cosell who turned me against the
tube; it was "Captain Kangaroo." Sweet, wise, wonderful
Captain, with his funny friends, his clever gimmicks, and his
marvelous music, cast a spell on my children that has not
been broken to this day. Before my babies were old enough to
talk, they would sit in their jump seats in front of the television set and jabber back to Bunny Rabbit and Mr. Green-
jeans, and by the time they were toddlers they were spending
their entire morning with the Captain, "Mr. Rogers," the
gang on "Electric Company," and the crazy creatures on "Ses-
ame Street."

I didn't realize how addicted my kids had become to TV
until they started to school, and I had to register each of them
for the afternoon session of kindergarten lest they succumb to
withdrawal pains from missing their morning TV. They
didn't care about early-afternoon TV (they thought soap op-
eras were silly), and they were home from school in plenty of
time to catch their all-time favorite shows: "The Flintstones,"
"Road-Runner," and "The Mouseketeers."

But someplace along their childhood, the wonderful world
of television copped out . . . literally. By the time our eldest
was twelve, our kids had switched their allegiance from cartoons to crime. Fred Flintstone, Yogi Bear, and even Annette
Funicello were cast aside in favor of the cops on "Dragnet,"
"The FBI," "Adam-12," and "The Mod Squad."

"Since when are you kids allowed to watch 'The Mod
Squad'?" my husband shouted one evening when he came
home and found our kids glued to the tube, enthralled by the
screams of a blond-haired beauty who was kicking and snarling her way out of an attempted assault. "Who gave you permission to watch this show?"

"Mom did," one of the kids said innocently. "Just ask her."

My husband came out into the kitchen, shaking his head
in disbelief.

"Did you tell the kids they could watch 'The Mod Squad'?" he asked. "Don't you make any effort to monitor their TV viewing?"

"Of course I monitor their TV viewing," I said. "I just made them change the channel because they were being brainwashed by that awful 'Brady Bunch.'"

"You prefer 'The Mod Squad' to 'The Brady Bunch'?" he asked incredulously. "I don't believe this! 'The Brady Bunch' is a wonderful family show!"

"'The Brady Bunch' may be a wonderful show," I said, "but it has nothing to do with family. It's full of propaganda!"

"Why do you say that?" he asked.

"Because the kids are always right and the mother is always wrong," I said, "and what's more, that fine, handsome husband of hers doesn't even have a job."

"What makes you think that?" asked my husband.

"Because he's always *there!*" I said. "The kids come home from school, and there's Dad, just waiting to listen to their woes. And where is Mom Brady? Out in the kitchen scrubbing mustard stains off the refrigerator? Or down in the laundry room trying to figure out why the washing machine is devouring the socks? No, she's sitting on the sofa, charming and gorgeous, trading quips with Dad. She doesn't work either. Our kids get the idea that parents have nothing else to do but sit around the living room and play 'parents.'"

"I don't get it," he said sincerely. "What else are you besides a parent?"

"I'm the maid!" I said, waving a dishrag in his face. "Give me an Alice and I too can sit around the living room and listen to our kids, or even watch TV with them. How can I monitor the kids' TV viewing when I never get out of this kitchen?"

"You're right," he said contritely. "It is ridiculous to expect you to run into the family room every thirty minutes to check the TV. We will have to do something about that."

And he did. He moved the television out into the kitchen. "This is a great idea!" he said, as he settled the television set on the kitchen counter. "Since our kids insist on eating while they are watching TV, this will keep the cookie crumbs and cola bottles out of the family room!"

He was right. We no longer had food in the family room, but we didn't have kids there, either. They were all crowded into the kitchen, where I had to try to prepare dinner to the accompaniment of televised police sirens or, worse, the "soothing sounds" of "American Bandstand."

While we no longer had crumbs under our sofa cushions, we now had something more frustrating: jelly in our TV transistors . . . along with spilled milk, pizza crusts, popcorn, and, in one unexplainable incident, an entire portion of fried liver. The kids could not seem to get through a meal, or even a snack, without spilling, dropping, pushing, or shoving something into the TV set.

But I'll say this for that television set; it didn't take all that abuse lying down. It fought back. When Tim inadvertently jabbed the TV antenna with his fork, the antenna retaliated by poking Tim in the eye. And when Peg carelessly slapped the set with a wet dishrag while wiping off the counter, the TV slapped back with an electrical shock. But it was not until Patrick spilled ice-cold lemonade down the back of the set that the TV wreaked its worst revenge: It shrieked one last battle cry, and died.

You cannot appreciate what a crisis this caused until you realize that this was our one and only television set. Suddenly finding themselves without a boob tube, our kids went into a state of shock. They wandered around for weeks, listless and disoriented. They didn't know what to do with themselves. Some of them, in desperation, took to reading books; others, more desperate and evidently becoming mentally disturbed, cleaned up their rooms. The eldest went so far as to go out and find a part-time job. I knew we had reached the breaking point one evening when I found the older kids discussing Solzhenitsyn and the little kids outside playing kick-the-can.

"That settles it," I told my husband. "We're going to have to get another television set."

"Why?" he said. "The kids don't seem to miss it, and I certainly don't miss it. The shows this fall are worse than ever!"

"Oh, there are *some* worthwhile productions on television," I said. "I miss the Boston Pops, and the tennis tournaments, and the news specials. But what I really miss are the commercials."

"You miss the commercials?" he asked with a laugh. "For heaven's sake, why?"

"Because nothing gets done around here anymore," I said truthfully. "You don't understand our kids; for years they have programmed themselves to do all their chores and their homework during the TV commercials. With nobody to say: 'We pause now for the following messages,' they don't know it's time to do the dishes!"

So we bought a new TV set and just in time, too. The actor's strike was underway and the networks were so desperate they reran Donna Reed.

27

Curfews for Young Adults

"I feel like I'm living in a men's locker room," said my daughter Mary when she came down to breakfast.

"Why is that?" I asked. "Have Tim and Pat been using bad language?"

"It's not Tim and Pat," she said, "and it's not language. It's Mike and Jim and the way they dress or, more accurately, the way they don't dress. Would you please tell those incredible hulks that this is not a fraternity house or a Marine barracks? Those two have been home for three days, and I have yet to see them in anything but their underwear. They sleep in their underwear; they work out in their underwear; I came downstairs at midnight to get a glass of milk, and they were eating in their underwear. It's like living in a Fruit-of-the-Loom commercial. Don't those guys own any clothes?"

"I'll say they do!" said her younger sister, Peg, as she pulled on a pair of socks she had just brought up from the laundry room. "No wonder they have to run around in their underwear; all their clothes are in the wash. I've never seen so many dirty clothes! I hate to tell you this, Mom, but that laundry room is a disaster area."

"So is this kitchen," I sighed. "I don't think the boys have stopped eating since they came home. I wish they would at least stack their dishes in the dishwasher."

You might think that after all these years of living with a houseful of kids that I would be used to a crowded laundry room and a cluttered kitchen, but in the few months since our four older sons moved out, I had been spoiled by a "relative" orderliness which can only be appreciated by a mother whose family has decreased from ten kids to six kids.

Over two decades ago, when I had given birth to four sons in four years, I had been warned: "When they leave home, it will probably be bing-bing-bing-bing, one a year." Incredibly, when the time came, they all left the nest in the same year. Our first-born got married, another moved into a bachelor apartment, a third went away to college, and a fourth joined the Marines. I was in a state of shock, not so much from loneliness, for there were six more siblings at home, but rather from the sudden change in "the environment."

With four stereos not only turned off but actually carted away, the noise level dropped to almost bearable. Our food bill was cut in half; our closet space increased tenfold. My husband rejoiced to find his shower once again poured forth hot water and, glory be!, he even had clean towels!

Everybody in the family commented on The Changes.

"Hey," said Peg one morning shortly after Jim had left for

the Marines, "I didn't know this laundry room had a tile floor! I always thought it was carpeted in dirty denim."

"You're thinking of the bathroom," said her sister Ann.

"No, I'm not," said Peg. "That's carpeted in wet towels."

"Not anymore, it isn't," said Mary. "Have you noticed how neat the bathroom is now, with the basketball gone from the bathtub, and the magazines missing from under the counter? There's even soap in the soap dish, instead of cigarette ashes."

"It's the refrigerator that gets to me," said Ann. "I opened it this morning to get a glass of milk, and guess what?"

"What?" I asked.

"I got a glass of milk! There were three quarts in there, and not one of them was empty!"

"That's nothing," said her brother Tim. "I opened the freezer yesterday and found a carton of ice cream that hadn't even been opened! I've never seen ice cream in our freezer before."

"That's because ice cream never got as far as the freezer before," said Mary. "The boys always ate it the minute Mom brought it home."

For the next few months we couldn't believe the cleanliness. I would lift up a sofa cushion and find . . . no sweat socks! I would look under a bed and see . . . space! I would come down to the kitchen in the morning and find . . . no beer cans, no dirty ashtrays, no pizza crusts!

But most incredible of all was my car. It was there. It looked so strange, just sitting there in the driveway, with nobody revving the motor, ready to zoom off on yet another errand, another spree. It looked almost pathetic, like a little dog waiting for its master to come out and play.

It didn't have to wait long.

With her four brothers gone, Mary suddenly realized that the impossible had occurred: her turn had come! The weekend was upon her, and there was no Lee, John, Mike, or Jim to pull rank on her. The car was hers!

Despite the fact that Mary had had her license for two years, I had never had to worry about her driving at night because, with four older brothers vying for the car, Mary had never had a chance to drive at night, or even much during the day. Thus we had been able to avoid the question of her keeping a "driver's curfew."

A "driver's curfew" at our house is thirty minutes later than a regular curfew, thereby giving the "driver" time to take everybody else home.

But the first Saturday night Mary took the car, she sailed out the door shouting: "Bye! See you at one-thirty!"

"Wait a minute!" I yelled. "Come back here. What do you mean one-thirty? Your curfew is midnight!"

"Have you forgotten, Mother?" she said sweetly. "I turned eighteen; my regular curfew is now one o'clock, and since I'm driving . . ."

"What makes you think your regular curfew is one o'clock?" I asked.

"Well, the boys got a one o'clock when they turned eighteen!" she said.

"But they are boys!" I cried.

"So what's the difference?" she asked.

"Mary," I replied patiently, "if you can't understand the difference between a boy driving around late at night and a girl driving around late at night, then you are too ignorant to be going out at all!"

"Oh, Mother, don't be a chauvinist," said Mary. "Don't you believe in equal rights?"

"If I believed in equal rights, Mary," I said, "I would be in the other room watching TV and pretending not to hear this conversation, and your father would be out here arguing with you! I do not intend to treat you like I would treat a boy!"

"I just want you to treat me like an adult!" she said.

"This will come as a surprise to you, Mary, but I am an adult. And I would not dream of driving alone in the wee hours of the morning. Why, if I did, I'd either be arrested for soliciting or committed for senility!"

"But I won't be alone," she argued. "I'll be with my friends."

"But you'll be alone after you take them home," I said, "and that's just too late for you to drive alone."

"I'll tell you what, Mom," said Mary, sounding exactly like her older brothers when they are about to con me into something, "we'll compromise. If you give in on the 1 A.M. curfew, I'll give in on the driver's curfew. How's that? May I stay out till one? My friends are really going to think you are weird, making us end the evening so early."

"Twelve-thirty," I conceded. "But that's it."

"Twelve forty-five?" she pleaded.

"Twelve-fifteen?" suggested her father from the living room, "or do you want to quit while you're ahead?"

"Okay, twelve-thirty," she said. "And I promise I won't be one minute late."

And she wasn't. She was, in fact, twenty-five minutes early.

"What are you doing home so soon?" I asked her when she came in shortly after midnight. "I thought you were going to stay out till twelve-thirty?"

"I was," she said with a sigh. "But all the other kids had to be in by midnight. Boy, there are some weird parents in this neighborhood!"

The question of curfews did not come up again until Mike's college vacation coincided with Jim's Marine liberty. The first weekend they were home, I didn't even think about a curfew. They were both adults, one seriously studying prelaw, the other pursuing a successful career in the military.

It never occurred to me to tell them what time they had to be in . . . until they didn't come in.

They had gone to a twilight movie, to catch the "before six" discount prices and, for some reason, I was sure they would be home for dinner.

"How could they be home for dinner?" my husband asked sensibly, when we sat down to eat at six-thirty. "The movie didn't start till five-fifteen."

"I'll keep their dinner warm," I said. "They'll be starved by the time they get home."

When they hadn't come in by nine o'clock, I concluded that they had gone out for a sandwich after the movie; they probably wouldn't be in till ten.

At eleven I turned on the porch light and went to bed.

At twelve I got up and decided to read awhile. I wasn't worried; they stayed out this late when they were seniors in high school! (Why do I have to remember when they were seniors in high school? Surely college-age kids wouldn't pull such pranks!)

At one-thirty I got up and walked the floor; that always used to work. A lot of Saturday nights I drew those kids home just by walking the floor.

When they hadn't come home by two-thirty, I woke my husband. He was furious, not because the boys weren't home, but because I woke him.

"For crying out loud!" he said. "You are not actually waiting up for those guys? They are men now! You don't worry about Mike when he is away at college or when Jim goes on leave in Singapore or Hong Kong." (Oh yeah?) "Why are you so worried now?"

"Because I'm a mother," I said, "and I don't have to have any other reason!"

At three-thirty Mike and Jim came home, laughing and talking and totally amazed that I had waited up for them.

They explained that after the movie they had stopped in to see their older brother John, had sent out for pizza, and spent the entire evening (evening? morning!) sitting around John's bachelor apartment catching each other up on each other's news.

"I know we can't impose a curfew on them," I told my husband at breakfast the next morning. "But I just can't go to sleep when my children are out at night, and that's true even with the children that are all grown up."

"I know, honey," he said, as well he should, after twenty-five years of putting up with my foibles. "I'll think of something to tell them."

And he did. That night at dinner my husband announced to our adult children:

"I'm not going to ask you guys to keep a curfew; after all, you are adults, and we trust you completely. What we can't trust is your mother's car. It's getting old and needs its rest. For that reason, we must insist that it come in early. So . . . I don't care how late you come in, but the car comes in at 1 A.M. Okay?"

Needless to say, our adult children agreed to abide by the car's curfew. Those kids may be all grown up, but they are evidently still not big enough to walk.

28

The "FIRSTS" Are the Worst

"I'm going to have a baby!" my friend Grace announced not long ago, and I nearly fell off my chair. Grace and her husband have been married over ten years, and I had long ago concluded that they would never have children. Grace is a successful lawyer, and I knew she loved her career; I also knew that she would not "take time out to have a child"; if she was committing herself to motherhood, it would be a 100 percent commitment.

"Frankly, I'm scared to death," she admitted. "I know so little about babies; I didn't have any younger siblings, and I never baby sat when I was a kid. I'm wondering if I'm competent to take care of a baby! Oh, Teresa, I'm not even sure I will like being a mother! Isn't that a terrible admission to make? But both Jim and I want at least three children, but having this first child really takes an act of faith!"

I agreed that having that first baby takes a real act of faith. What I didn't tell her was that parenthood is one long series of firsts, all requiring great acts of faith.

Nothing requires more total trust than the first time a mother leaves her new baby with a sitter. As every new mother knows, there is no one in the entire world competent enough to take care of her precious baby, and that includes precious baby's daddy.

I remember the first time I was forced to leave our first-born with a baby sitter. (I remember because nobody will let me forget it.) Lee was ten weeks old, and he and I had never been parted. I was so enchanted with my new role of mother, I didn't want to go anyplace and certainly not without him. I took him with me when I went shopping, when I went bowling, when I went to church, everyplace. On Saturday nights, if my husband and I went out to dinner or to a movie, we would take the baby along. (It must have marked him for life; he hasn't spent a Saturday night at home since.)

But the inevitable happened: an invitation came from one of my husband's most important clients; it was to a formal dinner party, and I knew that we would not only be expected to attend, we would be expected to attend unencumbered by a boisterous, and often damp, baby.

"Let's face it, Teresa," said my husband. "You have to re-sign yourself to the fact that at times Lee will have to be left with a sitter. Everybody leaves their babies with sitters; it's no big deal. We are beginning to look like a couple of nuts, drag-ging that kid with us everyplace. Why don't you call Susie What's-Her-Name next door and ask her if she can baby sit a week from Saturday?"

"Are you crazy?" I asked. "She's much too young!"

"She is?" he asked. "I thought she was a freshman at Duchesne College."

"She is," I said, "which means she is barely eighteen years old, a teenager, for heaven's sakes! You expect me to entrust my baby to a teenager?" (One of the drawbacks of being twenty-six years old is the fact that one can remember being a fun-loving teenager.) "We will have to look for a mature woman who knows something about children."

After spending the next ten days rejecting referrals from our physician, our friends, and various agencies, I told my husband that he would just have to go to the party alone. The day of the party had arrived, and I had still not approved a sitter.

"We are going to the party," he said firmly. "I arranged for a sitter; she will be here by six-thirty."

I was frantic, but I knew he was right. I would have to learn to entrust our baby to someone else's care.

As we got ready to leave that evening, I asked the sitter for the umpteenth time:

"Are you sure you know how to hold a tiny baby? Remember to support his neck. . . ."

"I think I know how to hold a baby," she interrupted. "I had six children of my own, you know."

But that was sometime ago, I thought to myself. Would she remember all the rules?

"Now, about feeding him," I said, "the formula's all made, but don't overheat the bottle, and don't force him to eat, but be sure he gets at least six ounces, and remember to burp him. . . ."

"I'll try to remember all that," she sighed.

"And don't lay him on the bed," I cautioned, "because he will scoot right off. Don't put him on the floor, either, because he'll surely catch cold."

"I'll hold him every minute he's not in his crib," she promised. "Don't worry so!"

"Here's the number of the pediatrician, the police, the fire
department, and the rescue squad," I said, "and here's where
we'll be. Don't hesitate to call if you have any questions."

"I won't have any questions!" she said impatiently. "Now
go to your party so I can spend some time with my grandson!"

"Yes, Mother," I said meekly, "and thanks for coming up
for the weekend."

Eventually we stopped imposing on my mother and
mother-in-law and learned to leave our children with "regular" baby sitters: teenagers, agency referrals, et cetera. But I
must admit, it was never easy for me to leave a brand-
new baby, for the first time, with a baby sitter, despite the
claims of Patrick's older siblings that, after Patrick was born, I
was so desperate to get away from them all I would cheerfully
leave them with any stranger who wandered in off the street.
That was ridiculous, of course; nobody but an idiot would
wander into our chaotic, noisy household, and when an occasional idiot did show up, I would always insist that she show
identification before I left her with the children.

Another traumatic "first" is that first time you let your toddler play outside unsupervised. (Please don't preach to me
about fenced-in yards; we had a yard with a six-foot fence; it
took our two-year-old almost ten minutes to scale it.) But a
mother can't "baby" her child forever; there comes a day
when she must trust him to stay out of the street and within
shouting distance. Even after having ten toddlers survive this
particular era, I still shudder when I see a preschooler whizz-
ing down a sidewalk (or worse, a driveway) on his tricycle.

Then, of course, there is that wonderful, awful day your
first child walks to school alone. In these days of bussing and
carpooling, I suppose few kindergartners are sent off on foot,
but ours were. And what an act of faith that took! This boy's

only a baby, for heaven's sakes! How can he possibly maneuver those long blocks, those busy streets, those monsters he will meet along the way? If you doubt that he will meet monsters, then you have never had a five-year-old try to wheedle you into driving him to school. I have had so many kids claim that "an elephant won't let me cross the street" or "a tiger chases me home every day!" or "there's a gorilla hiding up by Grady's house," I began to suspect that Marlin Perkins lived around the corner. But the monsters the child imagines are nothing compared to the dangers Mom anticipates, and this continues for each and every child she has, despite what my kids say about my shoving them out the door and shouting: "I don't care where you go, but don't come home before three o'clock!"

The worst "first" has to be the first time your child drives your car with you sitting beside him. (I do wish they would not call that the "death seat.") I have tried to avoid this traumatic "first" by refusing to get into a car with any of my children until they have taken Driver's Education and been duly licensed by the state of Nebraska. But it doesn't help, because if there is anything more nerve-racking than riding with a nervous teenager who is learning to drive, it is riding with a self-confident kid who thinks he knows everything about driving.

I wish I could say that the more a mother rides with her teenager, the easier it gets to climb into that car, but such is not the case. Every time I get into a car beside one of my driving children, I am convinced that before we travel six blocks we shall both be killed. Thus, whenever possible, I think up an excuse to stay home, and send my teenager to his doom alone. I am fully aware that his chances of having an accident will not be decreased by my absence, but since I am sure that he will have an accident with or without me, I would prefer that it be without me. After all, I have nine other children to think of. (And oh, dear God, nine other children who will all be driving someday!)

I had assumed that the last "first" would take place when the first-born announced that he had chosen his life's love and was going to get married. But I was wrong; the last first (or at least so far in my life) was a couple of years later when my daughter-in-law announced that she was going to have a baby. Good heavens! She is little more than a baby herself (grown up, of course; but I wonder!) how can she possibly be competent enough to care for a baby! Will she know how to hold a baby? How to bathe it and feed it? How to interpret its cries? Will she realize the dangers of open safety pins, scalding bathwater, sharp objects, a new father? If I could just move in with them for a few days . . . or weeks . . . or months. . . .

But, of course, that's impossible. Oh, dear, what an act of faith it takes to have that first grandchild!

29

The Perfect Mother!

"You are a perfect mother!" Patrick tells me periodically, which may explain to the rest of my children why I tend to be prejudiced toward Patrick. Of course, at age eleven, Patrick has not yet acquired the critical eye of the adolescent. Give him another couple of years and he will undoubtedly become vociferously aware of my imperfections.

Despite Patrick's enthusiastic endorsement, I am not a perfect mother. On a scale of 1 to 10, I probably rank about .00002, but it doesn't bother me, for after a century of motherhood, I have concluded that in all the world there has probably been only one truly perfect mother, and she had a couple of things going for her which I don't have. (1) She was unencumbered by the albatross of original sin, and (2) she only had one child. Furthermore, she was not inhibited by constant reminders from Dr. Spock, Hiam Ginott, and the Disciplinary Committee of the PTA. I may be an imperfect mother, but I am definitely in the majority.

I wasn't always an imperfect mother, however. There was one period in my maternal career when I was a total success. It was during my first pregnancy, and, in my enthusiastic anticipation of motherhood, I had purchased an entire layette, furniture and all, long before it was actually needed. The sight of all that "baby world" made me aware of my lack of experience in baby care, so I also purchased a doll and "practiced." I bathed that doll and changed it and fed it and rocked it, and do you know that kid never cried once?

I could hardly wait for the arrival of my own real baby; he would have blue eyes, curly hair, a perpetual smile, and he would be every bit as good as his plastic predecessor . . . sleep peacefully in his crib, drink all his milk, play quietly in his playpen, becharm the neighbors, and become the apple of his father's eye. As a mother, I was definitely going to be a "10."

Before the baby was three days old, I was already down to "2." Baby, born with blue eyes, no hair, and a perpetual scowl, had an aversion to his mother. He wailed like a banshee every time I picked him up. A nurse finally diagnosed his trouble: imminent whiplash. Every time I picked him up, Baby's head fell to a 45-degree angle. How was I to know that new babies have noodle necks?

Despite the fact that we constantly tried new formulas, Baby wouldn't eat or, when he did, he would quickly return it, ounce by sour ounce, over my shoulder. (In fact, the kid was a picky eater until he finally found the Golden Arches.)

Instead of sleeping peacefully in his crib, Baby spent his time contemplating ways to dismantle it, and we think he may have set some sort of record. At six weeks he had jammed the slide side; at three months he had bashed in the back panel; and we have yet to figure out how old he was when he crawled out of the crib and removed the castors. He considered his playpen a cage and howled bloody murder whenever he was incarcerated, a fact which somehow did not becharm the neighbors.

And the only thing he did to his father's eye was aim accurately at it whenever his daddy changed his diapers.

Fortunately, I did not have time to dwell on my failures with my first-born, for all too soon I was making mistakes with his baby brother, and within a year another brother, and twelve months later yet another brother. A mother who has four sons in four years soon forgets about striving for perfection . . . all she cares about is survival.

As my babies (six more were to follow the first four) grew into toddlers, I became more concerned about my inadequacies as a mother, due to the fact that we moved next door to the perfect mother. You know the kind: her babies never leaked; her toddlers never got dirty; her teenagers never caused her trouble. I hated her. While my toddlers were intent on destroying the neighborhood, hers were happily playing on their teeny trikes within the carefully set boundaries of their driveway.

Though my toddlers were notorious for surmounting our six-foot fence so they could run out into the street and chase cars, or go next door and hold the neighbors hostage, they were notable for one particular virtue. They shared. Like all kids in a big family, they had a kind of communistic outlook on life: Everything belongs to everybody. As all of their clothes and toys had been "handed down," nobody was ever sure just what belonged to whom, and they cheerfully shared everything from teething rings to tricycles to time.

I was so proud of this willingness to share, I didn't realize that it could be overdone until one morning when my four-

year-old son overdid it. Our toddlers had been playing in the
back yard with Mrs. Perfect's toddlers, and I was upstairs
changing the beds and keeping an eye on everybody through
the back-bedroom window.

Suddenly I realized that my four-year-old son was missing,
along with Mrs. Perfect's three-year-old daughter. I dashed
downstairs and found the two of them headed hand-in-hand
for the bathroom.

"Where are you going?" I asked my son.

"To the bathroom," he said without pausing.

"Uhhh . . . wait a minute, dear," I said. "I think it would
be better if Cindy goes first, and when she's through, you can
go."

"Oh that's okay, Mom," said my four-year-old son, "we'll
share!"

As I suspected she might, Mrs. Perfect soon heard of the
incident, and realizing the futility of trying to deal with "that
crazy mother with all those kids," she did us all a favor, and
moved.

When my children reached grade-school age, I once again
determined that I should strive for perfection . . . but how? I
couldn't drive a carpool; no car. I couldn't volunteer to work
at school: I still had too many babies at home. But I finally
found my niche . . . or more specifically, I was shoved into
my niche . . . as cub scout den mother.

It worked beautifully. Another mother, who did have a car
but not the time to be a den mother, offered to bring the boys
to my house each Tuesday while yet another mother offered
to take them home. As by this time I had five sons of my own,
having another six little boys around for one hour a week
didn't bother me a bit. In fact, I thoroughly enjoyed those
years, when I served successively as den mother for each of
our first four sons.

But then came my downfall. As I had been such a successful den mother, I mistakenly assumed I could also be a successful Blue Bird mother. Thus, when our daughter Mary reached the required age of seven and became a Blue Bird, I volunteered my services as scout mother.

Mary was horrified.

"*You* are going to be our scout mother?" she cried when I told her the news. "But *why?*"

"What do you mean: 'Why?'" I asked her. "I thought you'd be delighted!"

"All year long I've been waiting to go to Blue Bird meetings at somebody's house," she wailed, "and now I have to go to *our* house! That's no fun!"

"We'll make it fun, Mary," I promised her. "You'll see."

"Wellll . . . maybe," she agreed reluctantly. "But there have gotta be some changes made around here! For one thing, that sofa's gotta go; it's a disgrace. And look at those drapes! Can't we get new drapes? My friends will think we're weird!"

After a few more comments (à la her father the day before a dinner party), Mary and I compromised. The sofa and drapes would stay, but I promised to clean up the recreation room, where our meetings would be held. (And considering the normal condition of our rec room, that was quite a concession.)

Then Mary began to bring home suggestions from her little friends.

"Sara says she hopes we aren't going to play dumb baby games; we aren't, are we?" I promised: no baby games.

"Patty says she hopes we aren't gonna *make* things. That's so boring."

"Okay, no arts and crafts," I promised, mentally discarding my plans to use up all the craft material the cub scouts had ignored; happily, they had always been satisfied to spend their den meetings playing football.

"Cindy says we'd better not have any sing-alongs 'cause she has to save her voice for the opera."

"Cindy is going to be in the opera?" I asked in surprise.

"Yeah," said Mary. "She's got the juvenile lead again this year." Oh, *that* Cindy. Mrs. Perfect's daughter strikes again.

On Blue Bird Day, six little girls were deposited on my doorstep. Shy and silent, they obediently followed Mary downstairs to our rec room which I had, after all, painstakingly repainted and redecorated for the Big Blue Bird Year.

"It's hot down here," pouted a blue-eyed blonde, suddenly shedding her shy image. "Let's play outside."

"Oh, but we're going to play Bingo," I announced cheerfully. "We can't play Bingo outdoors. Now let's all sit down. . . ."

"*Bingo!*" shouted a redhead with fiery freckles. "Mary, you didn't tell us we're gonna have to play Bingo! We wanna play football! Hey, here's a football; stand back, Sara, and catch!"

"Let's play outside!" I said desperately, shoving the entire group out the back door. "You girls play . . . uh . . . football, and I'll fix the treats."

I was particularly proud of those treats. I, who seldom bake, had outdone myself with homemade chocolate eclairs.

"What's this thing?" one of the Blue Birds asked as the girls gathered round the picnic table for their treats.

"That's a chocolate eclair!" I said proudly. "And they are delicious."

"I don't like 'em," she said, pushing hers away, and like dominoes, the eclairs along the table followed suit.

"Me neither. . . . They taste funny. . . . They're sticky. . . ."

"When my mother was leader," said one of the Blue Birds, "she took us all to the circus and then bought us pizza."

Shut up, Cindy, and eat your eclair!

While I never made it as a Blue Bird Mother (Mary tolerated me through one year and then tactfully dropped out to save my face), I perfected one important talent during my tenure as a mother.

I am a superior . . . maybe even excellent . . . sack-lunch packer.

In the two decades that my kids have been taking school lunches, I must have packed ten thousand of the blasted things, and while I am sick of it, I am also very good at it. However, my excellence comes not so much from practice as it does from obeying. . . . I always do what I am told.

Despite the fact that I start each morning with the announcement: "This is not a restaurant; there are no menus. You may not get what you want but you're gonna take what you get!", I still get orders.

"Peanut butter and jelly? Oh no! Why can't we ever have cheese and mustard?" one will cry, totally forgetting that yesterday he had cheese and mustard and complained because it wasn't peanut butter and jelly.

"Is that grape jelly?" asks another. "Yecchhh! Don't we have any strawberry?"

"Leave the jelly off mine, will ya, Mom? And be sure to salt the peanut butter!" Another voice heard from.

"I just want half a sandwich," says a fourth luncher. "I have to eat fast so I can play soccer."

"Gimme two sandwiches," says a fifth. "I'm always starved by noon."

I have learned not only to make the proper sandwich, but also to make the sandwich properly. Sandwiches must be cut diagonally, as square-cut sandwiches are considered "hokey" (whatever that means). Also, the bread must be white, and fresh . . . not frozen; frozen bread makes soggy sandwiches. Homemade bread is *verboten*: it crumbles.

The sandwiches must be placed, singly, in clear plastic,

locktop or flip-top bags, wax paper being for peasants, I guess.
("It falls apart," and "you can't see through it," and "it makes
the bread taste yecchhy.")

The sack itself is also important; it must be a No. 8, store-
bought, brown paper bag. I once made the mistake of using
left-over grocery sacks and the kids had a fit.

"We can't take our lunch in those!" they yelled. "They've
been *used;* all the kids will think we're poor!"

The sack must be packed just so: fruit on the bottom so it
won't squash the sandwich; dessert on top so it can be eaten
first (?); an absolute must is a small white paper napkin. If I
dare use the large, luxurious paper napkins, I am told: "We
can't take those; all the kids will think we're rich!"

Over the years I have not only learned to pack ten lunches
while simultaneously cooking twelve breakfasts, but I have
also trained myself to remember who likes which jelly or jam,
who wants half a sandwich and who wants two sandwiches,
and who wants the chocolate Oreo and who the vanilla. As a
consequence, the kids never complain, and I have become
quite proud of my own little talent.

Until yesterday.

As the kids were picking up their lunches and filing out
the door, I gave Patrick a quick kiss and said: "You're a good
little boy, Patrick; enjoy your lunch."

"Oh, I'm not gonna be eating this, Mom," said Patrick
brightly. "I'm gonna trade with my friend, Joey. His Mom
makes fresh-baked cookies every day for his lunch, and he
told me if I let him play with my football he'd trade lunches
with me today. Isn't that neat; I can hardly wait!"

"Don't tell me; let me guess," I said. "Does Joey have a
sister named Cindy?"

"Yeah!" said Patrick. "How did you know?"

It just figured.

30

Future Shock
Has Got Me Shook

I don't believe in reincarnation, but there has to be some explanation for the fact that I am in the wrong time slot. I must be. Why else would I freeze when I wear miniskirts, wince when I hear rock music, and find no humor at all in "Saturday Night Live"?

Could I have led a swinging life in some past existence and am now working off my purgatory? Not likely, for I cannot imagine myself swinging in *any* century, or even enduring in a time when there was no central heating, indoor plumbing, stovetop cooking, or Sinatra-on-Stereo. As for a past life, I would have hated wearing bustles or crinolines (much too cumbersome!) and rebelled at dancing the minuet (much too corny). On the other hand, I certainly don't belong in the fu-

UP A FAMILY TREE

ture. Nobody, but *nobody*, could talk me into spending six-teen hours a day in a skin-tight, one-piece space suit. I've watched those Buck Rogers-type television shows, and I *know* why they need such long commercials.

No, I'm in the right century all right, but maybe I'm in the wrong generation. This occurred to me the other night, when my husband and I were watching "Hart to Hart" on televi-sion.

"I just realized what I don't like about this show," I told him.

"What don't you like about it?" he asked, somewhat sur-prised, as we watch it every week.

"There's something wrong with Jonathan and Jennifer Hart," I said.

"What's wrong with them?" he asked.

"They're not Nick and Nora Charles!" I said, remembering William Powell and Myrna Loy in that Dashiell Hammett classic *Thin Man* series. "Even in the 'modern' version, with Peter Lawford and Phyllis Kirk, there was witty dialogue along with a mystery to be solved. On "Hart to Hart," all there is, is kissy-kissy; I don't know how Jonathan and Jen-nifer ever find time to solve the murder, what with all that smooching."

I am not much of a television fan, but my husband enjoys a good detective series or mystery play, and since I enjoy my husband, I sit in the same room and read a book while he watches TV. The other night one of his favorite shows was on, and I found myself glancing up from my book occa-sionally to see what was going on.

What was going on shouldn't have been.

"Do I have an evil mind," I said sarcastically, "or is it true that every time I have looked at that TV screen I have seen a couple in bed together, but it's never the same couple? Or sometimes it's half the same couple . . . with somebody else's other half. What is this show, anyway? A sex marathon? I thought it was supposed to be a mystery."

"It is," yawned my husband, who, like most husbands, watches TV for sedation rather than entertainment, "the mystery is: who is married to whom? But I lost track about three wife-swaps back. You might as well turn it off." My husband is ready to give up on TV. He has never forgiven them for taking off those "entertaining" and "enjoyable" rip-roaring, bloodletting, gut-tearing, shoot-em-ups.

"Whatever is the world coming to?" my grandmother used to ask, and then she copped out and went to heaven so she wouldn't have to stay around and see just what the world came to, which is too bad, because if my grandma could have stayed around, the world just might not have come to it.

I know there is supposed to be a "generation gap," but the gap between my parents' generation and my own was a tiny crevice compared to the grand canyon that exists between my generation and my kids'.

Alfred Lord Tennyson warned us that "the old order changeth" and Alvin Toffler prepared us for "future shock," but neither of them could have predicted the shocking manner in which today's kids have changed the old order. Just consider some conversations in 1951, as compared to a similar situation thirty years later:

1951: "Mother, Joe just called me and asked me to the football game and to a party at Mimi Brown's afterward. We'll be doubling with Mimi and Hank and I'll be home by midnight. Is that okay?"

1981: "I'm goin' out with the gang; don't wait up."

1951: "Gee, Mom, that dinner smells good; is it meat loaf? My favorite! Thanks!"

1981: "Meat loaf again? How come we can't go to McDonald's?"

1951:   "Dad, is it okay if I use the money from my paper route to buy a bike?"

1981:   "Say, Dad, I'm gonna be sixteen tomorrow; how about springing a sports car for your favorite son?"

1951:   "Hey, kids, guess what? Mom and Dad are going to take us to Colorado this summer? Isn't that terrific?"

1981:   "A family trip to Colorado? Do I have to go?"

1951:   "I have to write a book report on *Jane Eyre*; thank heavens I saw the movie!"

1981:   "I have to write a report on the miniseries "Centennial"; do you think I can get away with reading the book instead?"

1951:   "Now, Daddy, I know you are worried about your little daughter moving into her own apartment, but, after all, I'm twenty-three years old and I'll be sharing expenses with Mary Ellen."

1981:   "Don't hassle me, Daddy. I'm getting my own place and that's that. After all, I'm a grown woman now, almost eighteen years old. And you won't have to worry about me; I'll be sharing expenses with Paul."

1951:   "Dad, could I possibly borrow two hundred dollars for next semester's college tuition?"

1981:   "Dad, could I possibly borrow two hundred dollars for next semester's textbooks?"

1951:   ". . . and he insists on opening the door for me, and holding my coat, and lighting my cigarette. What a nice guy!"

1981:   ". . . and he insists on opening the door for me, and holding my coat, and he even smokes cigarettes. What a weirdo!"

1951:   "Sir, I have been dating your daughter for two years now, I have my law degree, and am an associate in an established law firm. I would like your permission to ask your daughter to marry me."

1981:   *"Marry* her? *Why?"*

Actually, today's young people aren't really that bad. Stupid, maybe, but not bad. Of course, some of them do get a little carried away, "doing their own thing," whatever that is. (And whatever that is, I'd just as soon not know, thank you.)

As a consequence, modern parents are sometimes put on the spot when friends ask about their teenagers or young adult offspring. In such cases, I follow the course of the majestic mehitabel, the feline heroine of Don Marquis' classic *archy and mehitabel*. archy you remember, is a cockroach who comes out at night, jumps on his boss's typewriter, and relates the saga of his feline friend, mehitabel. Because archy is so small, he cannot reach the shift key, so the entire book is written in lower case, with no punctuation and no caps, thus mehitabel is not even allowed a capitalized name.

But this bothers mehitabel not a bit, for she is a most confident creature. mehitabel claims to be the reincarnation of Cleopatra, the famous Queen of Egypt, and she does, in fact, lead a very Cleopatran life, going out every night, carrying on with first one tom and then another, but always responsibly bearing her litter of kittens, whose existence she then blithely ignores. When her friends inquire about her current offspring, mehitabel innocently replies: "What kittens?"

My sentiments, exactly. When people ask me about my own adult children, I simply remark: "What kittens?"

Not that my kids are all that off-base, at least compared to some kittens I know.

Take my friend Freda, for example. Freda took a page from mehitabel long ago when her own son, Herbie, upon graduating from a very expensive Ivy League college, tore up his diploma, ran off to Africa, and joined the Foreign Legion. This was hardly something Freda cared to discuss, so, when well-meaning friends inquired about Herbie, Freda simply said: "He's in the military."

I wish Tish Baldrige would update her etiquette book with a chapter on how to answer well-meaning queries about our adult children who are "doing their own thing." Until Tish has time, I offer here a few suggestions for such answers:

If someone asks about your child, and:

He has dropped out of school, can't hold a job, and spends all day watching TV: "He's in the entertainment field."

He's in jail: "He is studying prison reform."

He goes to the race track every day: "He's in investments."

She's sharing an apartment with some clod who has no intention of marrying her and lets her foot all the bills: "She's studying Home Economics."

She has totaled her secondhand Chevy, torn out the transmission on your Olds, and borrowed her grandfather's Cadillac just long enough to ram it into a brick wall: "She's selling cars for General Motors."

He renounced the Draft, stole your car, and took off for Canada: "He is working on various projects with the FBI."

I suppose it would be simpler if parents would just quit fudging and admit, when they are asked about a "wayward" child:

"My kid's crazy; how's yours?"

But who's to say what's crazy?

Perhaps the kid who rejects the American way will work wonders in the Third World. And the kid who spends all his time tinkering with cars just might invent a fuel-free engine.

The fact is, kids of every generation have, at one time or another, marched to a different drummer, but most of us eventually got back into step. (. . . and walked into the wrong time slot?)

Who knows? Maybe today's kids will continue to march to a different drummer, change the course of the parade, and lead us all into a better world.

On the other hand, has anybody ever thought to check the credentials of the drummer?

31

Epilogue

"If you had it to do over, knowing what you know now, would you have ten children? Would you space them differently? Would you raise them differently?"

I have been asked those questions at least a hundred times in the past couple of years, and in keeping with my philosophy that variety is spicier than veracity, I have given a hundred different answers . . . none of which was Yes or No.

I wouldn't dare give a Yes or No answer to such questions. They're like that all-time classic: "If anything happened to your spouse, would you remarry?" Either way, you can't win.

If I said, "Yes, if I had it to do over, I would have ten children," I would be bombarded with arguments from ecologists on overpopulation and pollution; sociologists would remind me of crowded classrooms and unemployment; and economists would tell me I couldn't afford to feed ten children today. (I couldn't afford to feed them yesterday, either.)

On the other hand, if I said, "No, if I had it to do over, I would not have ten children," my kids would kill me.

Actually, it's not *what* I know now, but rather *who* I know now, that would be the deciding factor.

If I were starting my family today, knowing what I know now about colicky babies and toddler tantrums and grade-school pranks and the terrible, troublesome teens, and taking into consideration the high cost of living, and environmental concerns and energy crises, I would heartily agree that it would be absolutely insane to have ten children. Then I would go right ahead and have Lee, John, Michael, Jim, Mary, Dan, Peggy, Ann, Tim, and Patrick because I cannot imagine life without them (or perhaps because I *can* imagine life without them), and no matter how many times you count them, they still add up to ten.

Would I space them differently? Good heavens, No. I didn't start till I was twenty-six; if I had spaced them any farther apart, I would be having babies into my sixties or, worse, I couldn't have had Peg, Ann, Tim, and Pat, and that would have been terrible!

Having ten children in twelve years only seems insane to someone who hasn't tried it. As I look back on it (and the older I get, the easier it is to look back), our kids were perfectly spaced. Everybody was in diapers at the same time; everybody was on tricycles at the same time; everybody went off to school at the same time. Well, maybe not everybody, but it seemed so at the time. We didn't have to spend the first ten years putting the crib up and taking it down again; the crib was a permanent fixture, as were the high chair, the playpen, and the wall-to-wall toys. Nor have we spent the school years worrying about such things as carpools (we *are* a carpool), or winter coats and ice skates and spring jackets and Halloween costumes because there's always one "just about your size" in the front-hall closet. We don't have to keep up with the sophisticated subjects our kids are taking in school because there is always a sibling who remembers the course from last year. No, I wouldn't space my children differently. Kids are easier when they are annuals.

"But isn't it outrageously expensive to have so many kids in college at the same time?" Someone asked my husband that question recently, and after he paused a moment, his eyes lit up and he replied:

"So that's where they are! I wondered where those rascals went!"

He was kidding, of course. He knows which of our kids are in college. At least I think he knows; I'm almost sure I've told him that Mike, Mary, and Dan are at the university. Or is it John, Mary, and Dan? Or is it John, Mary, and Mike? Well, *somebody's* at the university. And if all those checks I've been writing aren't going for tuition and housing, then I now own a substantial portion of the University of Nebraska!

"But won't it be very hard for you when all the children have left the nest?" deserves only one answer from a parent of ten: "Is that a threat or a promise?"

If I had it to do over, would I raise them differently?

Yes, because every mother makes mistakes and it would be foolish not to rectify them.

If I had it to do over, I'd yell less and touch more. Yelling accomplishes nothing but a sore throat (Mother's), for kids have audometers which automatically turn off the moment a mother's voice reaches a certain decibel level. The louder she yells the less they hear.

Touching is so important, whether it be a gentle swat on the padded bottom of a stubborn two-year-old, a spontaneous hug for an exuberant ten-year-old, or the mere touch of hand to the cheek of a troubled teenager. Yes, I think I would touch my children more, though I might vary the procedures occasionally, to hug the babies and swat the teenagers.

If I had it to do over, I would spend more time reading aloud to my children, so they would become familiar with the classics, and so they would remember their mother's voice saying something other than: "It's time to get up!"

If I had it to do over, I would do it more slowly; I would take life at a more leisurely pace. While I have been rushing around the house, cleaning and cooking and searching and scolding, my kids have been growing up. Why didn't I take time out to watch?

If I had it to do over, I would never tell my children to "stay out of the living room" or "stay off the lawn" or "don't use the good dishes" or "don't touch my best towels," for this is their home, and no guests will ever be more important than my children.

If I had it to do over, I would spend more time with my children, listening to them, laughing with them, loving them . . . if I had it to do over.

If I had it to do over? What am I saying? With ten children, I *am* doing it over, and over, and over. . . .

Teresa Bloomingdale, author of the best-selling *I Should Have Seen It Coming when the Rabbit Died*, is the wife of attorney A. Lee Bloomingdale and the mother of seven boys and three girls, ranging in age from pre-teen to past-twenty. In addition to writing a weekly syndicated column, she has published articles in *Good Housekeeping*, *McCall's*, and other leading magazines and journals. She is a frequent book-reviewer and sought-after guest lecturer. She resides with her family in Omaha, Nebraska.